Walter A. Rodney

WALTER A. RODNEY
A Promise of Revolution

Edited by CLAIRMONT CHUNG

MONTHLY REVIEW PRESS

New York

Library of Congress Cataloging-in-Publication Data
Walter A. Rodney, a promise of revolution / edited by Clairmont Chung.
    p. cm.
  Includes bibliographical references and index.
  ISBN 978-1-58367-328-7 (pbk. : alk. paper) — ISBN 978-1-58367-329-4
(cloth : alk. paper) 1. Rodney, Walter. 2. Historians—Guyana—Biography.
3. Political activists—Guyana—Biography. 4. Pan-Africanism. 5. Black
power. 6. Africa—Politics and government—1960- 7. Blacks—Intellectual
life. I. Chung, Clairmont.
  DT19.7.R62W33 2012
  960.072'02—dc23
                          2012036818

Monthly Review Press
146 West 29th Street, Suite 6W
New York, New York 10001

www.monthlyreview.org

5 4 3 2 1

CONTENTS

To the voices included here
and all involved in struggle everywhere.

ACKNOWLEDGMENTS

The name Walter Rodney acted like a magnet for people who wanted to say something about him or contribute in any way to advance this book project. Many of them appeared in the film, and I thank them here and continue to thank them for all their efforts. Those who did not make an appearance in the film are equally important, and in many cases more so.

My desire to share the importance of Dr. Walter Rodney has kept this project going. Hubert Rodney believed in the project. Both he and Edward Rodney reminded me of the seriousness needed to attach to this and any project on Walter Rodney.

I thank all those who allowed me to use their words. I thank my immediate and extended family for understanding and for their support. I give a special thanks to my wife, Leslyn, and two daughters, Maya Nyani and Amali Naja, who helped with the transcriptions.

ABBREVIATIONS

ANC	African National Congress
CSM	Caribbean Single Market
CSME	Caribbean Single Market Economy
FRELIMO	Liberation Front of Mozambique
GDF	Guyana Defence Force
IBW	Institute of the Black World
IMF	International Monetary Fund
NJAC	National Joint Action Committee
NJM	New Jewel Movement
PNC	People's National Congress
PPP	People's Progressive Party
SOAS	School of Oriental and African Studies
TANU	Tanganyika African National Union
UNITA	National Union for the Total Independence of Angola
USARF	United Students African Revolutionary Front
WPA	Working People's Alliance

BIOGRAPHICAL TIMELINE

1942   Walter Rodney is born in Georgetown, Guyana, on March 23, 1942.

1953   Rodney wins a County Scholarship to attend Queen's College, a secondary school in Georgetown. It was a momentous year in that it was the first time County Scholarships were available to working-class boys. It was also the first year of full adult suffrage, and after the first exercise of that vote, British troops intervened to abort the democratic process.

1960   Rodney chooses to attend the University College of the West Indies (later known as the University of the West Indies) after winning an Open Scholarship. He is active in student government and campaigns on the island with the People's National Party in support of the West Indies Federation, which was a plan to unify the Caribbean into a single government. He visits the United States, Cuba, and Czechoslovakia before graduation.

1963   Rodney graduates with a first-class honors degree in history. He wins an Open Scholarship to the School of Oriental and African Studies in London. He joins the study group headed by C. L. R. James.

1965   Rodney marries Patricia Henry in London.

1966   At the age of twenty-four, Rodney is awarded a Ph.D. with honors in African History. His son Shaka is born about the same time. He leaves for Tanzania to lecture at the University College of East Africa, Dar es Salaam, which later became the University of Dar es Salaam.

1968   Rodney returns to Jamaica as a lecturer. He lectures on and off campus. After ten months he leaves to attend the Congress of Black Writers in Montreal and is barred from returning to Jamaica. The "Rodney Riots" erupt in Kingston and spread throughout the island. He returns to the University of Dar es Salaam and continues to lead debates on and off campus as in Jamaica. His daughter Kanini is born.

1969   Rodney's first book, *The Groundings with My Brothers*, is published. It is a collection of speeches given in Jamaica and in Montreal in which Rodney applies Black Power to a Caribbean context.

1970   His doctoral dissertation is published by Oxford University Press under the title *A History of the Upper Guinea Coast, 1545–1800*. It is rated by academics as his best history book. He continues to write and produces numerous papers, pamphlets, and editorials. His daughter Asha is born.

1972   He publishes his best-known book, *How Europe Underdeveloped Africa*. The book is one of the first to describe Europe's involvement as actively engaged in the underdevelopment of Africa as opposed to the usual position of underdevelopment through benign neglect.

1974   Rodney returns to Guyana to take up an appointment as Professor of History at the University of Guyana. The government then rescinds the appointment. Rodney remains in Guyana, joining the newly formed political group, the Working People's Alliance.

1979   Rodney is arrested for arson after the Ministry of National Development has been burned to the ground. He is released on bail. As he has done everywhere, he gives lectures wherever he is asked and becomes a leading figure in the fight against the dictatorship of Forbes Burnham.

1980   Still on bail, he travels to Zimbabwe, via Tanzania, to attend the independence celebrations. His passport has been taken as part of the conditions of his bail. He returns to Guyana and is assassinated as a bomb explodes in his car on June 13. He is thirty-eight years old.

PREFACE

This book began as a series of interviews for a long overdue documentary film on renowned historian and activist, Dr. Walter Rodney. The documentary, *W.A.R. Stories: Walter Anthony Rodney*, was completed in 2009. Moving images of film and video come with some inherent limitations, however, and so the participants' spoken words have evolved into a book, in order to add some depth and width to the subject. The intent is to make the oral history part of the formal history.

The oral tradition remains the most popular way of sharing information, and the digital camera makes possible that which we always wanted: making stories and images travel together, and relatively cheaply as well. The words and images given to the project had to be sliced and diced in the interest of the "story." The documentary's editors and I took pieces of statements and put them in a context that we hope maintains their integrity.

Although this book aims to present the original context of the paticipants' statements, the reproduction of spoken words will by definition be different. Transcribed interviews miss the inflection and poetic nuance of the spoken answer. Yet power and beauty exist in the word itself. When you read this book, see it as an opportunity to add your own nuance, your own inflection, power, and beauty.

We have omitted in the text the questions participants were asked. With as learned a group as this, answers were often reshaped, going beyond the preconceived confines of a given question. We have maintained the order of the individual answers with minute adjustments to the narrative text in an attempt to capture as close as possible the vibe of what was said. If some paragraphs seem out of place or context, blame the interviewer. The few questions posed were often intended as a guide but sometimes did not work as such, but this often turned out to be to our benefit. We have kept some of the "you knows" toward maintaining the vibe. Even some of the repetitions remain because we believe they add texture. The speakers of these words had no opportunity to review what they said.

1—Clairmont Chung

I was thirteen, in 1971, when Dave (not his real name) passed through my street and said he had something for me. The next day he brought new copies of Frantz Fanon's *Black Skin, White Masks,*[1] and an anthology, *The Complete Works of Mao Tse Tung,* volume 1.[2] Dave had recently been deported from New York City. Occasionally, he would stop and talk. These were brief encounters on Main Street, just outside Tiger Bay in Georgetown, Guyana. He lived in Albouystown, South Georgetown, but used to visit someone in Tiger Bay.

I do not recall a lot of the details of the conversations, but I remember the books because Frantz Fanon added a dimension to my thinking that I never relinquished. *Black Skin, White Masks,* despite its simple title, was difficult. But I understood the main tenets on identity and neuroses that flow from oppression. The Mao volume was thick and difficult to traverse. I thought one day I would publish my own easy-to-read anthology. But those books led me to another by Fanon, *The Wretched of the Earth,* which I found easier. Dave and I must have talked about the Black Power movement in the United States. Dave dressed and looked like pictures I'd seen of Bobby Seale,[3] H. Rap Brown,[4] and the Soledad Brothers.[5] Our meetings made me feel close to that movement. That same year, 1971, Walter Rodney published a tribute article to a Soledad Brother, "George Jackson: Black Revolutionary."[6] Much later, I realized that Dave most likely had encountered these books while in prison.[7] I do not recall any talk about Walter Rodney.

Each week I visited the John F. Kennedy Library on Main Street. I wanted to know everything about America and African people in America, because that was where I was headed. Abroad, I had a chance at higher education. Guyana had no room for me, despite being the least geographically dense country in the world. I was not an academic standout. Even if I had applied myself, I would still probably need membership in the PNC to realize my full potential. Back then, members of the ruling People's National Congress[8] enjoyed first choice for state resources, which ranged from higher education to food.

This was a different Guyana from the 1950s (then British Guiana), the one in which Rodney came of age. The Cold War was still raging in 1971, as it was during Rodney's coming of age, but gone were the earlier possibilities discussed by the political elite: multiracial unity against colonialism, race-blind distribution of resources, and increased rights for the working class. There were early signs of unrest, like the split in 1955 of the African minority from the People's Progressive Party (PPP)[9] to form the predominantly African PNC. But it was nothing like the racial violence that would characterize the early 1960s. Rodney was abroad by then. Instead, we saw the rise of partisan politics, race-conscious decision making at all levels, a negotiated independence, and the rise of the doctrine of paramountcy in the PNC to a national goal. Rodney had been sensitized to the basic principles regarding the rights of working people at a very early age. His father, Percival Rodney, an active member of the PPP, played a significant part in molding his worldview. His older brother, Edward, also contributed much then and up until Walter's death. But the political situation into which Rodney would return in Guyana in the mid-1970s was very different, without the promise it once held. This was no shock to him. He had kept abreast of developments. Contributors to this volume like

Rupert Roopnaraine and Robert Moore, in particular, help paint a clearer picture of this earlier period of Rodney's life.

Dave and I never had a chance to discuss the books before he left. Later, we ran into each other on Fulton Street, in Brooklyn, New York. This was the early 1980s. We still wore our Afros, but the movement in the United States was long dormant. The leading figures were dead, locked up, or exiled. One of the leaders of that movement, Amiri Baraka, points out in his interview here: "They were then harassed and murdered and locked up, some still in prison all these years."

Dave's books were not my first exposure to the movement. I was aware of Malcolm X's[10] assassination and later Dr. King's murder,[11] the Kennedys,[12] and Stokely Carmichael's visit to Guyana in 1970. Carmichael was a student leader in the civil rights movement. He had marched with Dr. Martin Luther King, Jr. Carmichael would have been fresh from the Congress of Black Writers that Walter Rodney attended in Montreal in October 1968. After the Congress, Rodney was barred from reentering Jamaica and from his teaching job at the University of the West Indies in Mona. Carmichael was himself barred from several places, including England and his own home, Trinidad and Tobago. Another Congress attendee, Robert Hill, is included in these pages and recounts that time. Amiri Baraka was invited but did not attend the Congress due to some legal issues stemming from the Newark riots of 1967.

There is a shared history between that Congress, the ensuing student takeover at George William University in Montreal,[13] and the mutiny in Trinidad.[14] I followed the mutiny and the resulting treason trial in 1970. Rodney's exclusion from Jamaica on his return from the Congress had precipitated the "Rodney Riots."[15] I wanted to but couldn't attend Carmichael's lecture. It was reserved for upper-class students—that is, the students in higher forms. My sister attended. I grilled her about it. She felt Carmichael had a problem explaining Black Power to Guyanese, given that the local conflict was between East Indians and Africans. Later I learned that, unlike Rodney, Carmichael had excluded East Indians from his definition.

That summer, after Carmichael's visit, I read another novel that had a serious impact on my thinking and much later would help me in my understanding of Rodney. *The Young Warriors* by V. S. Reid was not part of the reading list at Queen's College. It was the coming-of-age story of five teenage Maroon boys in eighteenth-century Jamaica. Surprisingly, the book was on the reading list for that other middle-class school, Bishops' High School, which was the female equivalent of Queen's College. Africans that escaped the plantations formed independent communities and were referred to as Maroons, runaways. On one of those lazy August days, stuck at home, probably being punished for something I didn't do, I reluctantly started the book, which belonged to another sister. I finished it that day. I knew those boys were the boys I could be. I jumped straight out of my bed and stood up when Chief Phillip of Mountain Top, at a meeting of his war captains in the Council House, said, "Some of us may die. Maroons have never been afraid of dying. But we will never be dishonoured. Swear by your swords!" So began a long sojourn, off and on, into the dense forest of Caribbean history and Caribbean struggles for freedom.

Then, around 1974, I heard Bob Marley's LP, *Catch a Fire,* for the first time. We seemed to walk differently afterward, with chest out and a swing of the torso with different levels of swing to suit the occasion. The same as after reading about Chief Phillip. But it was Marley's *Rastaman Vibration* in 1976 that transformed me. I believe it transformed the whole region—the world. Rodney's impact in the region was evident in Marley and the Wailers: a new consciousness. After expulsion from Jamaica, Rodney went to Tanzania. Issa Shivji covers some of that period here. Walter Rodney would have returned to Guyana from Tanzania by then, 1974–75.

We burned a hole through that Marley album in Bushman's, a bar above the location where Walter Rodney and the Working People's Alliance would later open their office, in Queen Street, Tiger Bay. Rodney and I never met. I attended St. Stephen's Primary School as did he—at different times, of course. I also attended Queen's College, as did he, but with significantly less notoriety.

Sometimes, I would see him drive by as I and the rest of the lonely souls, the street-corner regulars, stood watch at Cemetery Road and Freeman Street, which was the entrance to East La Penitence, South Georgetown. On that corner, the major events of world history were discussed, and some not so major. Sometimes others would point and say there goes Walter Rodney, but not much more. One afternoon, another corner-boy took me to the Rodneys' home. He said there would be drumming and poetry. Rodney was out.

I visited the Tiger Bay office of the WPA. I passed by a few more times, but never saw Rodney. I learned a little more about him and his time in Jamaica. Some of the elders around Tiger Bay spoke about him. A few were founding members of the Movement Against Oppression (MAO), inactive by then but formed to address the rise in summary executions and other police violence against neighborhood youth. The number of executions that continued to grow through that entire period has not stopped, and remains uncounted and unaccounted today.

I left Guyana in 1978. I got to New York in 1979 and missed the period of civil rebellion that threatened to topple Forbes Burnham and the PNC regime. Some believe it succeeded. A lot of what is recorded here deepens our understanding of that period. But it's much more than that. Rodney and the Working People's Alliance, the party he helped found, led that rebellion. Then Rodney was assassinated in 1980. Before long, Maurice Bishop was executed in Grenada in 1983. Bishop led the New Jewel Movement (NJM) in Grenada and seized power from the repressive government of Eric Gairy in 1979. That same year, in Nicaragua, the Sandinistas led by Daniel Ortega overthrew the repressive dynasty of Anastasio Somoza. Progressive forces were advancing, but Bishop's death shook me back to the reality, and made clear the real danger of pursuing a path of self-determination. Just like Rodney's expulsion from Jamaica, the two deaths, of Rodney and Bishop, marked a turning point in progressive politics in the Caribbean but in the opposite direction. An attempt had been made on Bishop's life just six days after Rodney's death. A bomb exploded on a stage he was to share with other NJM leaders and killed three young women instead. It took them three more years.

I was living in Harlem by 1983, and attending meetings on Pan-African issues. "The Ladder,"[16] at the corner of Adam Clayton Powell and Dr. Martin Luther King Jr. Boulevards, was still a popular, if not daily, attraction and Ed "Porkchop" Davis[17] a popular speaker. It was not unusual to run into Dr. Ben-Jochannan[18] or Elombe Brath[19] on the street. The whole length of Dr. Martin Luther King Jr. Boulevard [125th Street] was a learning experience and captured by the title "University on the Corner of Lenox Avenue," or UCLA.[20] Lenox Avenue was by then Malcolm X Boulevard. It seemed no one could possibly know more African history than Dr. Ben or more about current affairs in Africa than Elombe Brath. All this was happening as the crack and cocaine epidemic consumed us in another kind of captivity.

Then there were the lectures at Convent Avenue Baptist Church on 145th Street in Harlem, the *Free Your African Mind* series, and other talks on campus. People like Dr. Van Sertima,[21] Dr. Tony Martin,[22] Dr. Scobie,[23] and Dr. Jeffries[24] came. Some would make references to Walter Rodney's books and in particular *How Europe Underdeveloped Africa*. WPA activist Lincoln Van Sluytman on two occasions brought VHS tapes of Walter Rodney speaking. I don't recall much detail of what Rodney said, but in some deep recess, something stuck: self-emancipation.

My early attempts to understand self-emancipation went very slowly. I understood that emancipation would come by our own hands. After all, Cuffy in Berbice,[25] L'Ouverture[26] forty years later, and captured Africans, the French, the Americans—people everywhere, it seemed—attempted at some level to emancipate themselves. What frustrated me about those attempts was the idea that something so right could actually fail and the idea of the right timing. How does one know the right time for revolution? The more I listened to Walter Rodney on self-emancipation and, in spite of his clarity on our history, the idea that we would spontaneously rise up and overcome our immediate confines sounded too biblical. I do not know if he would have conceived of such a confrontation as nonviolent. But he did say, in Guyana, that if we should reach that stage of violence, it would not be the fault of the people but that of those in power who failed to recognize the currents of history and foreclosed all other avenues of peaceful change. Marley joined the international debate with

Emancipate yourself from mental slavery
None but ourselves can free our minds
Have no fear in atomic energy
'Cause none of them can stop the time.[27]

It was prophetic. But how would we know we were emancipated? What role does armed struggle play? Would the army cooperate and not open fire? History is littered with examples where the army chose the side of government, its benefactor, against the people. The incident at Kent State in May 1970 comes to mind, where the National Guard shot and killed four students. At Jackson State College ten days later, local police killed two students. The Detroit Rebellion in 1967 resulted in forty-three deaths and over four hundred wounded after the National Guard intervened. Newark, New Jersey, and Watts in Los Angeles were some of the major battles between the people and the state that resulted in similar numbers of deaths and substantial property damage.

Or would it be like those officers in 1970 Trinidad who refused to fire and instead considered the overthrow of Eric Williams's People's National Movement (PNM) government? After all, Rodney was himself victimized by the army and its generals in Guyana.

On August 18th, 2012, security forces in Linden, Guyana, killed three unarmed men protesting a plan to increase electricity rates. One of the signs in the ensuing protest read, "People's Power No Dictator." Walter was still alive. In May 2010 over seventy Jamaicans died (a disputed number believed to be much higher) as a result of an attempt by Jamaican soldiers and police to capture known drug lord Christopher "Dudus" Coke. In Guyana, it is believed that a few hundred, mostly young men of African descent, were killed in a war for drug and political turf initiated by drug lord Roger Khan. Both Dudus Coke of Jamaica and Roger Khan of Guyana are now in U. S. prisons. But more important, both alleged that they were working with the government in various activities including crime fighting. How does one respond to that level of terror? Do we respond with peaceful protest? We ought to know the lengths to which governments will go to eliminate threats and retain power.

In talk a given in January of 1981,[28] C. L. R. James lamented Rodney's death and seemed to decry something impetuous about Rodney. James was at the Montreal Congress of Black Writers in 1968, too. He was a mentor to Rodney. I wanted to jump to Rodney's defense, because there was no guideline as to the right time to move, no known sign to indicate that it was time. James spoke like a prophet. Rodney needed to wait, and when the time was right, it would reveal itself. Incredible, I thought. A man held in such high esteem by so many, Rodney too, would say stuff like that. This Georgetown, Guyana, was not the bushes and creeks of Berbice. Where does one hide in the city? This was not the mountains of Jamaica and Haiti. James advises that in these circumstances, one leave the country and live in exile. In our interview included here, Rupert Roopnaraine likens James's comments to that of a mourning father in pain on his son's passing.

The prophetess of self-emancipation, Harriet Tubman, was much more decisive. She moved fearlessly and at great personal risk. A former captive and in danger of recapture while on a mission, she indicated she would have freed many more had they known they were slaves. She may have been the model for Rodney. She did not wait for any sign or major rebellion. Others who had the luxury of time and celebrity would debate the merits of revolutionary action and the means.

I decided to take another look at the old man, James, and came away feeling that no one knew as much as he about European contributions to history and philosophy. He located the notion of self-emancipation in Europe in the Age of Enlightenment.[29] The period when writers like Rousseau, Diderot, Pascal, and Voltaire were, according to James, raising the issue of human rights, and Europeans envisaged peons rising up and liberating themselves. He saw the effect of that period on Europe, France in particular, and on Haiti, too. James himself had written about self-emancipation, and most notably, *The Black Jacobins*, about the Haitian Revolution.

Captive laborers in the extended empire did not have the luxury of writing or reading about self-emancipation. They lived it, under threat of certain death rather than imprisonment. There was no active militia looking to kill Diderot as was the case with rebelling slaves. Rodney too was in hiding. So while Diderot and company were writing, Cuffy and company in Berbice were living revolution. At about the same time, in the early 1760s, George Washington, the first president of the United States, was a wanted man. Washington was not exactly captive. In fact, he owned captives. But the point is as much about colonial, as well as class domination: war and revolution. The end of both ought to have meant the end of captive labor. We know differently now. Americans lived it. Citizens of France lived it. L'Ouverture and Chief Phillip fought for it against those same enlightened nations. There was no time to read Diderot. This was something else. Enlightenment did not extend to captive labor in the colonies in sufficient quantity to free them. Though possibly from the same eternal source, this idea of freedom was arrived at independently among Africans in the New World. They would have to free themselves.

Violent revolution is what Fanon contemplated against colonialism. He surmised that any real liberation had to be by bloodshed as a way of cleansing oneself of the colonial self-image that was itself imposed by force, by bloodshed. Rodney would later refer to negotiated independence as "briefcase independence."[30]

After one seizes power then one has to face the question of government. Cuffy died long before the final nail in the coffin of the Berbice revolution. Part of the Berbice emancipation challenge was whether to set up a state retaining the structure of the Dutch or to retire to the rain forest and set up a different experiment: a Maroon experiment. The former required captive labor because, or so it was reasoned, it had to compete in the global market of that time. Cuffy contemplated the need for the skills and markets of the Dutch after emancipation to ensure the survival of a viable Berbice. In his letters to the Dutch governor, Wolfert Van Hoogenheim,[31] Cuffy contemplated living together. But without any commitment from Hoogenheim, he decided on separate and apart. But it is unclear whether he seriously contemplated a Maroon existence, though the Maroon communities predated the start of the 1763 revolution and continued many years afterward. I use "revolution"with my own definition: it took place where an organized system of government and defense existed and was destroyed. Cuffy became "Governor of the Negroes of Berbice," not a "Chief of the Maroons." James made clear his sentiment that it was the Maroons who were the real liberators of Saint-Domingue, not those seeking to expel the planters and retain a semblance of the planter system. That never really happened. It did not happen in Berbice, either. The Dutch regrouped and retook Berbice. In Haiti, the captives defeated the French but had to pay compensation to the landowners, and in many ways are still paying today. Issa Shivji's contribution in this book, though he makes no such analysis, allows us to compare Mugabe and Zimbabwe with L'Ouverture and Haiti on the question of negotiated independence. The control and redistribution of the land for economic advance is still an issue. Today we struggle with preservation and conservation of the land under attack from corporate aggression and with a view of environmental protection as part of our survival.

Unlike Cuffy, some of his generals preferred the Maroon existence. They outlasted Cuffy and frustrated the Dutch. The Dutch were well aware of the problems a Maroon community posed to continued exploitation of free African labor. Captured Africans routinely escaped and found refuge in nearby Maroon communities. In Guyana, Maroons would clear land, build whole villages surrounded by moats filled with sharp, pointed stakes. The bridges across the moats were hidden underwater. A nighttime attack was particularly treacherous. Besides, any attack would probably be ambushed long before it arrived. Non-disclosure of the village location was the one oath of a warrior. During the revolution, a campaign of raids and fire bombings were launched from these strongholds, which destroyed the infrastructure and freed the planters' most valuable asset: captive labor.[32] The Dutch buried their silver outside of their houses to avoid losing it to either rampaging freedom fighters or the heat of their burning homes. In Jamaica, in 1739, the British signed a treaty to end the first Maroon war, which offered land and autonomy to Maroons in exchange for the return of future runaways.

In Jamaica, Rodney spent time among the remaining Maroon communities and their modern-day equivalent, the Rastafari community. He did this while a UWI student in the early 1960s and later as faculty, until his expulsion in late 1968. This was primarily a learning experience. After all, these were communities seeking an existence outside the framework of the state and the ever-present institutions of commerce and exploitation.

In London, Rodney came into the James "circle,"[33] and they must have debated this notion of the timing, the means, and the operating system. Only twenty-one, he continued to hone his already significant communicating skills. He tested his ideas in Hyde Park, as well as in the living rooms of participants in the circle. During this period, he was under constant surveillance. As was the case for Tubman, the risk was significant. If the north was not "free," Tubman would have created a Maroon community. She needed a place to run to and which was defendable. Under Chief Phillip, Maroon children of Mountain Top grew up in a state of preparedness for war. It was primarily a war of defense.

In London, to avoid police scrutiny, the James circle rode separately to Hyde Park and took different routes back to the flat to discuss the day's events. Even Rodney's research trips to libraries on the European mainland attracted surveillance. It was not the bush of Berbice, but self-preservation instincts persuaded a cautious approach.

Tanzania, seen as free from international surveillance, provided a reprieve for Rodney. After all, "fugitives" from that peculiar concept,

American justice, were welcomed, along with freedom fighters from all over the world. Ironically, Guyana at that time was also seen as a place of refuge from "justice."[34] Tanzania's position in the struggle for Southern Africa sharpened Rodney's understanding of self-emancipation, but some conflict may have developed with James's notion of waiting for the spontaneous moment. Even Tanzania's president, Mwalimu Julius Nyerere, weighed in on Rodney's position on armed struggle. Issa Shivji talks about that in this book. I believe that even Rodney may have struggled with this issue. No amount of scholarship, no amount of notoriety, can prepare anyone to recognize the moment to act and by what means. Maroon movements around the world were primarily defensive and rarely attacked the enemy—and almost never head-on. In times of war, they waged guerilla warfare.

In Guyana, according to some, Rodney grew impatient, but in addition to the impatience there was a sense of moving the pieces forward and perhaps inspiring the moment. This was coupled with a commitment to take as many risks as any of the other comrades. Many have since criticized Rodney and called him reckless, and worse. But they are missing something very central: Rodney had no intention of seeking power for himself. He had no facility for risking his life to gain power and then responding with the same system of governance, albeit with new window dressing.

One has to understand youth growing up in and around Albouystown, Tiger Bay, West Kingston, parts of Brooklyn, and Soweto to understand Rodney's next move. They risked their lives every day to feed themselves, doing whatever they could. There might be other ways of making a living. Barred from working at the University of Guyana, Rodney found other ways of survival.

Rodney was intellectual, yet accessible. He was academic, yet grounded. But he was much more. At heart he was rude, a rude-boy.[35] He was Maroon, and unless we understand that, we will forever misunderstand him and have to tiptoe around the question of armed struggle among others. I use "Maroon" to describe him, not because he inherited any blood from Maroon ancestry, but because he inherited an understanding that something different had to happen. He saw that in Jamaica's Rastafari movement. It's where problem-solving hits the road. He was always prepared for struggle and in a constant state of readiness to defend. He wasn't about to wait too long for any explosion of popular will. He was under attack. But frontal attack on the state was probably remote. If that is interpreted as violent, then we may have missed the entire meaning and importance of what it means to be the wretched of the earth.

The only way we can exclude armed struggle from the equation of freedom, equality, and justice is to be separated from the history of the Cuffys, L'Ouvertures, and Chief Phillips of this world, from Harriet Tubman and George Washington. So we look at our youth today and lament their walk, talk, music, and the hang of their jeans. We despair at the results of contact with the criminal justice system. Unsustainable numbers are in jail, and we wonder how this is possible in this century. Captive laborers today include those behind prison walls working for free or close to it. If you visit courtrooms across the world and see our youth enter, shackled at the hands and feet, you would understand what is coming. This is what Fanon warned would happen. They are the ones best prepared to challenge power, with only their chains to lose.

At another time they would have come of age with clearly defined roles and skills. We look at Rodney and we know that, like him, these are warriors, seemingly out of place and time, underutilized, and without clearly defined roles set at the rites of passage, stripped of opportunity, but in a fight to change that—a fight for their lives.

Rodney had followed all the other rules. James had cautioned that people must be "educated" in order to exercise people's power. Rodney spent considerable time doing just that. He wrote books to speed up the process and lectured wherever he stood.

As I write, in Egypt Hosni Mubarak has been forced out of office by popular revolt, tried, and convicted. The military seeks to impose its will. One gets the sense the will of people is set on a larger goal, and all as a result of seemingly spontaneous people's action. Tahrir Square has become a battleground and a point of reference. A piece of all of us is camped on this historic ground.

In New York, Wall Street has been shaken, as in the time of George Washington, it is *occupied*,[36] and many symbols of power, worldwide, are coming under attack. My friend Dave is back in Guyana: deported again.

The people of Linden, Guyana, are under a state of undeclared martial law because they dared to challenge the government's decision to raise electricity rates.

Self-emancipation according to C. L. R. James is what comes after you've done a sufficient amount of work in communicating with people about their condition. That condition is the one created by the exploitation of labor for profit. The challenge to capitalism and its bankers today now seems similar to the challenge to the Dutch West India Company,[37] a challenge to greed. It's a challenge to the dehumanization of people by corporations, which share all the rights of the people but are not subject to limitations and punishment. The work came easily to Walter Rodney because he was always a communicator.

This anthology is about that work. This collection of interviews was created while making a documentary film on Walter Rodney's life. The interviews are not analyses of Hegelian and Marxian enlightened ideas as they apply to today's struggle. They are about how one lives and dies when one struggles. The stories themselves are Hegelian, Marxian, and existential. They do not contain predictions based on careful analysis of history. They are not an extrapolation of what Rodney would have done were he here today. This is oral history: living history.

The documentary *W.A.R. Stories: Walter Anthony Rodney* ends with Rupert Roopnaraine, Walter's right-hand man, lamenting the absence of Walter Rodney's work in schools in Guyana. Roopnaraine need not worry, because every day some group of parents, mostly women, are shutting school doors in protest against the conditions of the school, or marching for clean water or against violence. We have to see the connection and support it. They may not have read Rodney or James or Diderot, but the activism is no less valid. Rodney lives because they live.

During the making of the film while doing research in Guyana, I sat with a group "grounding"—that is, telling stories about our experiences. I had just finished telling a story about Jamaica. Unexpectedly, one and then another, two friends about to start at the local university, asked me whether I had read *The Young Warriors*. They asked me whether Maroons still existed in Jamaica. Bearing in mind it's a novel and fictional, the question was understandable. I told them about the current Maroon communities and urged them to visit. I had been searching for a copy of the book. That they had read it gave me a real sense of inter-generational bonding.

That was three years ago. Recently, I ordered a copy. It took three months to arrive and was returned to sender twice. The sender's address was in Sweden. Walter had instructed in *Groundings with My Brothers*[38] that a revolutionary should always have a good book in his backpack. While waiting to board the bus in New York City, a youngster approached me and said, "That's a really good book." Not sure of what he said at first, I responded, "What?" He repeated his statement. The line started to move, and I told him I had read *The Young Warriors* when I was thirteen or fourteen. As he took his seat in the bus, I asked where he learned of the book. He said, "In school, in Jamaica." He looked about fourteen. He added that he would really like to reread it and asked where he could get a copy. When I walked off that bus, my shoulders were broader and I was swinging from a far place. This book too would fit easily in any backpack.

Activists complained for thirty years under the dictatorship of Hosni Mubarak about apathy, particularly of the young. While watching coverage of the Egyptian revolution, I saw a young teen-ager coming of age, standing in Tahrir Square[39] with a sign that shouted, "We will live in dignity or die here!" He also looked like fourteen. Maybe now we see that this is not something one plans and schedules. The stories in this volume tell us what one has to do. One prepares. One educates. One waits. One demands dignity. One demands humanity. Chief Phillip's Maroons were never conquered, never dishonored. They lost some battles. They had fled the plantation and resolved to live free or die.

Walter Rodney's father, Percival Edward Rodney, came from Berbice. A member of the family I interviewed for the documentary referred to that branch of the family as the Berbice Rodneys. I believe a part of what Walter brought was that spirit of the Berbice revolution. It was clear to me that he had much to do with the ideological development of the family, and most notably of Walter. It is that spirit that lives. It did not begin with Cuffy. It did not begin with Rodney. Walter has said in tribute, to all our families, "Humanity is not something one proves; one asserts it," and "People's power, no dictator." Walter Rodney is that boy standing in Tahrir Square. He is Dave. He is James. He is you: Chief Rodney, a young warrior. He is the promise of revolution.

2—Robert "Bobby" Moore

The first half of the 1950s brought V. J. Sanger Davies and Walter Rodney to Queen's College. For Mr. Sanger Davies, who arrived from the Gambia in 1953, it meant being principal of an awesomely prestigious high school (high schools based on the British grammar principle were often referred to as colleges), with an outstanding record of academic distinction among its graduates. Even those not academically inclined were noted for an urbane and easily recognized self-confidence. Leadership in many situations in Guyanese society was often accorded to graduates as a matter of course.

For Walter Rodney, being at Queen's College [1953–1960] meant a stellar cluster of academic, extracurricular, and athletic achievements. At the end of his Queen's career, an Open Scholarship took him to the University College of the West Indies (UCWI). There he gained a First-Class Honours in History and a towering reputation for public speaking and debating. Three years at the University of London followed, crowned by a doctoral thesis published in 1970, which flowered into a most provocative work titled *How Europe Underdeveloped Africa*.[1] The debate it generated is still going strong in both the Global North and South.

But to back up a little, when I joined the teaching staff at Queen's in October 1955, Walter was already being talked about by some of my colleagues. The more speculative ones were envisaging him as one of those students likely to raise the long-standing prestige of the school to an even higher level.

With two years at Queen's behind him, Walter had become noted for a sharply analytic mind and a rich vocabulary with which to express it. His stock of witty quotations, his own wit, and a lively body language kept the eyes and ears of those in his vicinity focused on him.

By the time I encountered Walter in the classroom, in the Upper Fourth Classical,[2] he had clearly enhanced his gift for leadership. His peers enjoyed his self-confidence, which did not come with arrogance. They bonded with his sense of humor. They were impressed by how much reading he had done and how much of it he could quote from memory. On top of all that, his teachers were clearly taken with his writing: lucid, concise, *questioning,* and flavored with the Rodney wit.

In 1956, the prescribed history syllabus for the Upper Fourth forms still focused on the British Empire, beginning with the sixteenth century and ending in the decade following the Second World War. That was definitely not my cup of tea. Besides, members of the Upper Fourth forms were hearing, with some excitement, that West Indian History already held pride of place at Mona, the UCWI campus. And they wanted to know why Queen's did not have that subject on its syllabus. That enlivened my resolve to see such a course established.

So I brought the principal into the picture. When I first approached him, he was bureaucratically cautious. He needed, he said, some sober time to think the matter through. But within a day he had his response ready. With his skill for holding opposites together in creative tension, he hit on a compromise that I could live with: "Teach West Indian history in the first and second terms; in the third term you can teach some aspect of British imperial history that does not raise your hackles or make the 'boys' switch off."

And so the saga began. In 1957, there was no history textbook of the West Indies suitable for those lively teenagers of the Upper Fourth forms. A very scholarly *History of The West Indies* did come out that year, but its style was much too magisterial to ignite the interest of students in their mid-teens. There were also some short histories of individual West Indian territories aimed at the middle sections of secondary schools, but the writing tended to be unprovocative. Clearly, my approach would need something new and different.

After much reflection, I realized that the notes I made at Dr. Elsa Goveia's lectures of 1953–54 at UCWI would be the best temporary substitute for a textbook. Dr. Goveia had much to recommend her to Queen's College students. She was Guyanese by birth and schooling. She was a convinced West Indian, eager to witness the creation of a unified West Indian political entity. A specialist on slavery in the West Indian context, Dr. Goveia focused on its psychological and sociological effects on the evolution of West Indian being and thinking. Significantly, her lectures also included the impact of East Indian indenture on the region, and, with brilliant insight, compared slavery and indenture as two powerful systems of oppression. This combination of approaches recommended her to Queen's College students, whether of African or Indian heritage. To crown it all, her lectures were unforgettable and profoundly awakening.

I had envisaged lecturing from my Mona [UCWI] notes, but Walter suggested that I lend my notes to student volunteers from the three classes, who could produce typed copies as a text resource. Some students from the Upper Fourth Modern proved most enthusiastic and joined the Upper Fourth Classical in this venture. Somewhat later, the Upper Fourth General came on board, led by a number of far-seeing individuals.

Thus, a small and excited group of students from the three Upper Fourth classes, led by Walter, set about to type the sections of Dr. Goveia's notes, and they found the process engaging and enlightening. Enthusiasm spread among students and staff alike, who became convinced that West Indian history would, sooner rather than later, find a place in the curriculum at Queen's.

As I hoped, the use of this course material enlivened classroom discussions of slavery, indenture, and their offshoots.

All this was right up Walter's street. He belonged to a generation that grew to maturity at a time when slavery was becoming a fit subject both for scholarly research and dinner conversation. Much the same was true for the Indians students, then at a healthy distance from the stigma of indenture. They were asserting the dignity of their heritage in India, a land of many great civilizations.

Discussions led to resource material beyond the lecture notes, as students eagerly tapped the scholarly resources of institutions such as the British Council and the United States Information Agency. In fact, the USIA became further engaged by bringing down works on Caribbean history by American academics for the boys.

Their growing skills and vibrant discussions inspired me to designate a class period for debating and public speaking that used and sharpened their research related to the course. Some students wanted to add a Saturday class to progress more quickly in public speaking. That was not officially endorsed, but I mentored several of them informally.

It goes without saying that Walter Rodney and a few others would emerge as strong performers in both the content and performance of debating.

Meanwhile, the class was moving more deeply into various aspects of slavery, as a fundamental aspect of their history. It was the 1950s, and, at the same time as this course, the world was becoming aware of the growing apartheid policies in South Africa. It was difficult for me not to notice that what was going on in South Africa amounted to a contemporary form of slavery, which governments in the West were doing their best to ignore. When I suggested this to the Upper Fourth Classical, there was an "aha" moment across most of the class. This gained credibility when we discussed how slavery means the absence of mobility and empowerment. There is disenfranchisement from voting and voice in society, as well as the inability to change status and move freely in the community. Apartheid demands the same things, supported by pass laws, racial disenfranchise, and enforced separation.

Just then Trevor Huddleston's *Naught for Your Comfort*[3] was published, and I obtained a copy. This Anglican priest wrote clearly of the most fundamental aspects of apartheid and slavery when apartheid was being introduced. I passed it among interested students. When it returned, it was no longer a book but a series of chunks of printing held together loosely by a bit of glue, but I knew that it existed in its entirety within the boys.

This prompted me to speak to the principal for another update of the curriculum, in order to officially include apartheid. After a long discussion, it was agreed that there could be a component on "the history of slavery in the Caribbean, and one of its modern equivalents," and that's how the study of apartheid worked itself into the 1957–58 curriculum.

As the course evolved, so did the debating. It grew from a class ritual to a serious ventilation of the issues involved and imbued the school's Debating Society with a new dynamism.

It goes without saying that Walter Rodney and a few others would emerge as strong performers in both the content and performance of debating.

It was such a hot topic that new resources emerged quickly. The British Council began to bring books and newspaper clippings that would prove to be excellent resources in contemporary thinking.

It was here that Walter's tremendous skills as a debater came to light, his probing of the issues and mastery of words that would draw audiences beyond the school. Teachers and senior public servants were among those who made Queen's their Friday night activity during the school year. They came primarily to hear Walter speak and to marvel at how the content and delivery were so masterly interwoven.

Walter would go on winning trophies as a debater. Just before he left for the University of the West Indies, he won the prestigious Patrick Dargan Cup, the highest national award for debating. He would carry these skills through UCWI years, debating for the university at competitions throughout North America.

One of the highlights of my teaching career was a book presented to me at the end of the 1957–58 school year. Unbeknownst to me, the boys had divided themselves into groups to write essays related to the course or their perspectives on life in Guyana following taking the course. They presented me with a book of essays that they had paid to have professionally bound as an expression of their appreciation and the way the course was presented.

There were many other personal connections to this class that evolved over time. The boys kept me informed of their academic success, professional careers, and personal achievements. Almost all of them went to university, where they became figures of note. Several became leaders across academic, professional, and sociopolitical fields at home and abroad and some contributed to the ending of apartheid.

Rodney's story unfolded in perhaps the most dramatic way, as the voice and views that were nurtured at Queen's College made their way across the world.

Queen's College has every right to be proud of this alumnus, whose impact is still being felt in places where social justice, human dignity, and human rights are respected or fought for.

3—Abbyssinian Carto

I have been living in Fort Greene, Brooklyn, for the last seven years.
I am an artist, and I got politically involved when I first came to the
United States. In Guyana, when I left, there was some amount of
political consciousness, but not formed in any direction. When I
first came to the States, I knew about slavery but not what it really
meant, even though Guyana and the rest of the Caribbean were slave
societies. It's amazing how ill-informed we are about its origins or its
impact, how little we know. We sort of treat it as a historic event and
not something that impacts all of our society and us as individuals.
When I came to the States, it was about learning how millions of
people were moved out of Africa and what this did to black people,
not only in terms of the decimation of Africa but also what happened to people once they arrived on this continent.

I looked at Western movies growing up, and I, like everyone
in the cinema, would cheer as the cavalry would be coming over
the hill to rescue those poor beleaguered white people attacked
by Indians. Then I came to live in this society and began to learn
the history of both slavery and what happened to Indians in this
country and the deliberate genocidal approach that Europeans had
toward any other race they met. Both in terms of what happened

in the Americas : like what happened to Indian people with Cortés[1] and the rest of them.

That really impacted me politically, and that is when I started to "dread" my hair. It did not come through religious conviction in Marcus Garvey or belief in Haile Selassie; it came because I wanted to be different and outside of that cultural influence. It was the first thing I thought about. That I would dread my hair and step away from a Western concept of how one should appear. And from that I became involved with a lot of groups, trade unions, fighting like Chávez[2] did with the Farm Workers Union out of California, and people from South America, whether from Chile or Colombia or Guatemala. I became loosely involved with those organizations here in the United States. I participated in anything that had to do with Congress or the United Nations or in the street to make people aware of what was going on in their own homeland. So there was a network where we supported each other. If there was something on Guyana, then they would send their representatives. Through that networking I began to build an international connection to people from other countries in a political situation similar to what Guyana was beginning to emerge into under the Burnham regime.[3] At that time Burnham was only beginning to formulate things, but there were troubling signs of what was about to emerge.

I had other friends, like my sister, who had gone back home after living here. But there were other people who were involved in MAO, Movement Against Oppression, which was a forerunner of the WPA that had been established because a lot of young black youth out of Tiger Bay had been killed by the police, execution-style. They formed that organization, lending political voice to these people.

I was here from 1972 to 1979 at art school but would go back during summer breaks. That is when I became involved with a number of things in the political movement in Guyana.

There was *Dayclean*, the organ of the WPA, which was not yet a political party but a pressure group. Around this time, Moses Bhagwan was jailed for publication of *Dayclean*, and I remember

going outside the jail in Camp Street to picket and demonstrate, my
first involvement.

Moses was in jail because *Dayclean* was deemed an illegal newspaper. There was a requirement for publication of any paper. Burnham
did not ban things, but he made things impossible. The fee to have a
publication was some 100,000 or 200,000 Guyana dollars. Then you
had to keep renewing, and we refused to pay any of this but continued publishing. Moses was arrested because the initial license was
under his name. WPA had their offices in Tiger Bay[4] at that time,
and I remember going there, writing up posters, and going outside
the Court to demonstrate. I had been involved in demonstrations
in the States against various things, but this was the first time I was
involved in Guyana in any form of public demonstration. This was
a new experience for me. It was quite interesting, because here in
the United States you interacted with people, particularly during
the time when some people were holdovers from the Vietnam War
and were very politically aware, and you were operating within this
large population. Out of it, there was some response when people
came by. But in Guyana it was different. Some people would come
by, some ignore you, and some were afraid to come forward. And
that got worse under Burnham. More and more people would be
afraid to come forward to express themselves, or give support, or
even to ask you questions in the event they were accused of being
anti-government. But this was an interesting period because it prepared me for that longer period when I would finally return.

It's hard to evaluate Black Power in Guyana, because when the
PNC came to power it was a sort of Black Power sort of thing, not in
a traditional sense. Burnham used it as an umbrella to galvanize support. Black people had been denied their own autonomy, their own
ownership of things, and access to power in any sort of fundamental
and concrete way. I think it found itself into Guyana because for the
first time we had a black government. Even though they only came
to power in the collusion with America's CIA, which financed them
with that strike, the longest strike we ever had in the Caribbean.[5]
It brought down the PPP. And the PNC in coalition with the UF,[6]

which allowed them to have a majority, came to have power. Black people did feel marginalized in the society from both the white colonial thing and also from Indian people, who were treated differently in terms of cultural things and access to finance. I think what was happening in the United States was registering there, too. The government used it as part of their political drive to galvanize the support of black people.

I finished school in 1979. And I returned, but then Burnham began to tighten. He began to create legislation both in terms of the powers of the state and police, and the referendum had already been formulated: the paramountcy of the PNC was one of the things. The party was going to become paramount over all government institutions.[7] Of course, it was cleverly done. Burnham was a politician, a very clever one. He was a lawyer. Someone said to me that he had met a leader from Africa who had said, "What you have to do is make things into law. Once you make something into law, it's the law." South Africa had the pass law. However heinous it was to the population, but it was the law. Once on the books, it's harder to fight it. Burnham understood that.

There was resistance by the WPA, which brought this matter to the forefront. One of the fortunate things key to WPA's role during this period was its multiracial makeup. The PPP, being an Indian party, though it may have had some Africans, and the PNC may have had some Indians, the majority of both parties were made of either Africans or Indians. Burnham had been very successful in marginalizing the PPP. There was always a question of this race thing, and the PPP also had intimidated the PPP to a large extent. They were sort of paralyzed and could not mobilize in any effective way against the state. The intervention of the WPA into that with a multiracial umbrella eased the way for the PPP in a lot of ways. It allowed them more flexibility, and we took the pressure off them. We began to question policies. There were black people like Walter, so you couldn't appeal to him to remain silent by saying, "We are black people, therefore don't say anything 'cause there are Indian people who can swamp us and eventually take over, and where would we be? We would be back where we started or worse." Our intervention into that was we would say no and fight against different things.

The Arnold Rampersaud case, which you may be familiar with, is one of the things Walter fought for. This Indian man, accused of killing a black policemen at a toll booth, was tried two times and was about to have a third trial. This was when Walter spoke out against it, using historic facts and also evidence in the case. I think the multiracialness of the WPA allowed us to intervene in a very profound way. If WPA was not present during that period of time, I do not know what direction the politics would have taken in Guyana. I believe we came at a very crucial time. Certainly we prevented what would have been a worse situation in terms of how the regime would have responded to the PPP, if they had decided to retaliate or assert themselves with their majority of Indian people.[8]

Those were very tense times. We were all under constant police surveillance. We knew that. Sometimes you can recognize it. But a lot of time the state had access to state apparatus and it would not be unusual for a Telecoms truck to be parked on your street or a Guyana Electricity Corporation truck to be parked on your street or outside your house, manned not by employees from those institutions but by the police. There were times when things were recognizable and other times when you wouldn't know. Burnham had a very extensive intelligence network. It was not to be underestimated. I don't believe anyone else in the Caribbean, any other government, had that type of intelligence network. It had to do with the fact that the party was based in a very grassroots way. So it would not be unusual for somebody who is a vendor, someone selling sweet mangoes, to be connected with them. Or someone just liming[9] on the corner, or bridge, working as an informant looking at your movements, when you are coming out or going in and so on.

During this tense period houses were constantly raided. You were constantly being stopped and searched with a lot of threats. By that time the death squad had been formed as part of the police force. It was not acknowledged, except by us, as being a death squad. They were referred to as "Special Branch" or something like that. But those who operated politically knew otherwise. They were there as a political instrument of the state. Even though a lot of times, when they were not dealing with us politically, they dealt with that petty criminal element on the fringes of society, who tended to operate at night. They were pursuing them and shooting them, and executing them, and brutalizing them in very terrible ways. So we constantly had a sense of being in a dangerous place. Because on any given day you never knew what would happen. I mean, there were people who had been arrested and badly beaten or someone had been killed; we know of incidents when people were killed, not WPA people, but people killed and a cutlass placed next to them. The police would drive around with these cutlasses in their vehicle and place them next to their victims and claim they had been attacked. So the danger of that happening was always there for us.

When National Development[10] burned down, I was staying at a house on Robb Street, which is like three blocks away from where it happened. I heard this loud explosion and then the skies lit up. There was a fire going on. It is always deceptive in Georgetown how far away fires are because when you see it you think it's closer than it really is. It happened in the morning, after midnight. It may have been around one or two in the morning. I went up to look at it, as did many people. In Guyana fires fascinate people and they came from all around, because fires were always good to them. It wasn't a political statement against the government. I think it's some primordial thing. Guyana has these wood buildings, and when we watch them go up in flames it's something we are tapping into, even though fires mean a loss to some person or persons.

But later on the following day, well, we found out that Burnham suspected the WPA was behind the arson. His orders were for the arrest of a number of us, the leadership. This included Walter, Rupert, and Omowale.[11] I suppose besides ordering the arrest, they were piecing together intelligence and noting that Walter had been seen here or there or whatever.

For me, personally, a good friend that I had not seen since school days, who had been at school here in the States, came to see me. She came to the place I was staying in Robb Street, opposite the Guiding Light, which is a known PNC place. That girl got into trouble because they were able to say her car was parked outside my place and what time she arrived and left. Her aunt was a minister in the government. To this day I've never seen her again. Nothing happened to her. But she was told to leave. So she left the country and went away. It became much tenser. The whole burning of the building intensified the oppression against us, because it was seen as a serious threat against Burnham, as it was. One could not take it lightly.

I never went into the courtroom when they were having the trial, because it was always crowded with a lot of people. Walter and the WPA had established a relationship with the population to a degree where people came out. There were always little crowds of people surrounding the courts, watching, listening, and talking politically about what was happening in the country, what the trial meant, if they felt Walter and Rupert and Omowale and others were guilty of the arson, what needed to be done. It was quite interesting for me because people were challenging the state in a certain way. Not in a frontline way of doing it, but if you listened to the conversations, this act as far as they were concerned was a correct act. Because we were doing something, we were moving in the direction of confronting the state. There was a lot of support in terms of how people felt. Again, you have to remember that the whole race thing that governs Guyana was hard for people. Because in terms of challenging Burnham, the PNC always said, "If it's not us it's them." So people may have felt some personal sense of loss, and if this thing did not go correctly they could end up being marginalized again in the society. I think the PNC certainly told its supporters and made that known publicly. But there was always a lot of tension. Of course, there were police outside the courts. Some were in plainclothes; after a while you'd recognize some of those people. You can see them listening and trying to ferret out what was being said.

They were freed on bail. That was the day they killed Father Darke. Because after they came out of the court—Rupert, Omowale, and Walter—there was a lot of cheering. The crowd had heard they were bailed and was ecstatic. They were walking down Brickdam with the crowd following behind, and as they were in front of St. Stanislaus [high school] going toward Brickdam police station, the thugs came out and started wading into the crowd and attacking, beating people. Martin Carter[12] was in the crowd. Martin subsequently wrote a poem about that. Father Darke got killed because they thought he was the publisher of the *Catholic Standard*. I can't remember now who the publisher was, but he was white too. Father Darke was a photographer. They didn't like photographers. Anybody who took photographs of breaking up meetings and stuff like that were the first to be attacked. Any documentation of the actions of the state was not to be tolerated. Even if you had a camera around your neck, not shooting anything, the police would come and either arrest you and take you away or physically take the camera. And that is how Father Darke was attacked and killed.

Again, it's interesting when reading Martin's poem. It's really interesting. What happens when you live in a society still in transition? Inasmuch as Guyana was still a slave society and we were in that colonial period, a level of calmness still existed within it, a structure of law and order and stuff like that. Enough so that I can even remember when you came to a major road [stop sign] and police were not around, you either stopped or touched the ground with your feet. This was supposed to pass as an excuse for stopping, but it sort of inculcated in you, in a certain way, that a certain order existed. That sudden eruption of violence when those thugs came out—and it was the House of Israel thugs[13]—these men were coming with sticks and one of them had the bayonet that killed Father Darke. In the midst of the event, it's almost like a surreal experience. It's like a slow motion thing where you can see everything. You can see the blade of grass. You can tell a leaf on a tree, you can tell the angle of the sun, or what is happening. Everything becomes so perfectly clear to you. That was the amazing thing about it. So in the midst of people running in different directions and trying to avoid being beaten and attacked, you see things unfolding.

That day, perhaps because it was House of Israel people, I was not zeroed in on, not targeted. So I was able look at things around me and see things happen. There were other times. I remember I was at a meeting[14] at Golden Grove and I saw a truck come up, a trailer, and it deposited a number of people. They came and started to tear into the middle of the crowd. The first thing they did was to try to grab the microphone and the speakers, but they were also beating people. The crowd ran. We had to defend our instruments and our things but also not break ourselves up into groups. Usually they would isolate you. If three or four people isolate you, then you have to consider making a run for it, jumping into somebody's yard, or running up the road or jumping into a canal. There are stories about people going through cane fields to get away. Usually if somebody in that neighborhood helps you, they know the cane fields, which are very complex structurally, how they are laid out. That's what helped Nigel[15] when he was chased that time on the West Coast. There were some people in that area who were able to guide him through, and if the assailants came into the cane fields, they would know what to do. But there were a number of times when I was caught and beaten.

I remember one day they broke up a demonstration we held outside the court, and I received a cut on my head. There was blood on my T-shirt. I had a white T-shirt. They released us that same day. But later on that afternoon there was a meeting on the mall.[16] I went to that meeting with the shirt. All those arrested earlier had returned for the meeting and were wearing the clothing that had been torn up and bloodstained. It was almost like one of Martin's poems, where he said, "You come with your banner...."[17] There was a really deep sense of this thing about struggle. It was more than a spiritual awakening for me. It is a spiritual awakening in a certain way, but it's more than taking a religious path, it's a very profound transformation that happens to you. It's where that understanding of life and death becomes so clear. Particularly when dealing with a state as this one, where we can die or be killed. As Mao said, "A revolution is not a tea party." It's when you challenge a state like that you become aware of the profound consequences and what can happen to you. And you are dealing with a state that has already shown what it can do, its level of violence, its capacity to kill. I don't think it's because we were brave people. I believe we just reached that point in our lives where we said we are not taking this anymore.

Even though we were constantly harassed, it was one of the things that we had to deal with. Whenever I was there in the market, whenever I was in Georgetown, running around, there was a sense of a center of myself, a proudness. Not that I am brave person, but that we were fighting this thing.

One of the things that always amazed me in Guyana was to see the actions of big men, men who have children, men I grew up respecting. Growing up, everybody who was senior to you was always called Mister. Any of my father's friends who came to the house had to be addressed as Mister. You couldn't call them by their names. Now, I was finding that these men or similar men were so afraid. They were afraid to take a *Dayclean*, to read it, because what if they are seen by somebody who reports them. They were afraid to stop to talk to you because you were a known WPA activist. The state had created that fear and sometimes it was not a matter of reacting violently against them. One of the most effective things that Burnham used was to take away people's jobs. Guyana is a small country. All of us are concentrated in a small region on the coast. When you take away someone's job, their capacity to feed or house their family, then it really frightened people. And there are not a lot of people who are going to say, "Well, I am going to fight them and take that risk."

I was always recognizable. They had a recognition handbook of known WPA activists. It was like a police dossier. It would have height, a description, age, what you looked like, and a photograph. They did not have my photograph, but I was always recognizable at demonstrations. We always had big cardboards with anti-government slogans. The understanding was, if the police came, we were to fold them up and, if there was a crowd, try to blend in with enough time to get away. But I was always a target. I couldn't hide; they would recognize me from a distance, whereas others could just blend in and disappear in the crowd. So a lot of the times I was targeted, beaten, and roughed up. I remember a meeting at the Mall[18] for which we did not have permission. And we had gone ahead. Walter had decided to hold the meeting in any case. The police appeared, and they threw tear gas, which broke up the meeting. People were running, because the tear gas burns your eyes and so on.

We had a WPA banner, and there were these Special Branch, riot-squad, guys. They are really a tough set of men when you have to confront them. I remember holding on to this banner and them pulling and us not releasing it. I remember deliberately not looking. I was at the front holding it. A TSU [Tactical Services Unit] man was at the other end. I did not want to make eye contact with him. I was not afraid. But I thought that if I looked at him, then he would retaliate much more. I was in defiance of him, of his execution of his duty. I don't know how he felt personally, his political thoughts. So I kept my eyes down, and they couldn't take it away from us. It wasn't that we were stronger than they were, but it was our determination to protect our rights. This piece of thing, just a banner, nothing significant to get beaten for, took on a larger significance. All of a sudden it became something larger that we wouldn't let them have. I remember one officer taking the gun butt; he had a long rifle, and hitting me on the side of my rib. But I still didn't release it. In the midst of which you don't really feel the blow. Of course, later I felt it. My ribs were sore for a few days.

There were different times when those different incidents came up. For example, we had a demonstration outside the court when Walter's trial was on. It had been going on for a couple of weeks. They had broken up the demonstration we had. Again, we were observing. We weren't disrupting traffic; we were not doing anything illegal. They sent in the thugs. They came in with batons swinging and were beating us up. I remember being pulled by this one policeman they called "Serpico": a tall, fine, "red" policeman.[19] He had a terrible reputation of killing people. He lashed me with the gun butt, grabbed me by the shirt, and pulled me toward a bus waiting up the road. He dragged me and threw me up against the bus and said he would shoot me. I told him to go on and shoot me. Again, this is not because I wasn't afraid or being brave. It was just that I had reached that point where I said, "If you want to kill me then go ahead and do it." And I told him, "You must be sure that I am dead, because I will come and look for you." They were shocked when you'd throw out this challenge to them and show you are not afraid. And at that instant, I was not. I mean, before the demonstration starts you know they're going to come and break it up. You have a certain amount of fear, because to get beaten or your head busted, or they break your arms or crack your ribs, you have fear. You have fear when you realize what it is to deal with a group of people intent on violence against you, when you have no way of defending yourself except putting up your hands to block things. They have guns. They have long batons and stuff like that. Then you are afraid, but in the midst of it, fear just completely leaves you.

Anyway, they put us in the bus and they drove up the East Bank and we were asking where they were taking us and they wouldn't tell us. There were probably about twenty-five of us in the bus, and we began singing and shouting through the window anti-government slogans and actually cursing Burnham, you know. We were some of the few people who could curse Burnham publicly and say what we felt about him. And they took us down into Mocha, a village on the East Bank[20] that is bordered by cane fields on both sides. There was a black village in Mocha, and the intention was that they had arranged with young people in the village or their supporters in the village that when we came off the bus, they would beat us. The only exit back out was this almost mile-long road bordered by canals on both sides, and cane fields. But we sort of organized ourselves when we came off the bus and found some pieces of wood and various things to arm ourselves with, because we were determined that we wouldn't run, but that we would stop and fight because we had women among the group, and there were younger people, teenage people that had come along for the demonstration. And a group of young people did come up threatening us, but because we were so determined and told them that we would fight them, I don't think they were into it, really. So, they never attacked us, and we made our way back to the public road and were able to catch cars to get back to Georgetown.

Walter had always said that there was possibility of this happening, that the state would try to kill him, that he had become the symbol. I mean, it was amazing to go to public meetings during this period of time and see black people and Indian people standing up together. For the first time they were listening and looking at each other as brothers, comrades, that there was some common bond. We come from different religions and different races and stuff like that, but we really are not different. We have the same concerns about ourselves, about our families and children. And about our own exploitation, which historically has gone from slavery to indenture to now. And you heard them discussing things. When Walter was reasoning with them, he had that way of, when he spoke, talking to them, taking their lives personally and identifying with them and seeing, listening, asking, "What are your fears as an Indian about black people? What are your fears about black people as an Indian?" He'd discuss where this fear comes from and how it had been used by both parties in terms of exploiting your loyalty to them and stuff like that. And Walter understood it—I mean, part of the thing of him doing that "history of the working people of Guyana"[21] was challenging this period. We'd be out there in meetings, not only in Georgetown but in other areas like Wismar, Berbice, up on the coast, East Coast, West Coast. And he would come back at the end of the day and have these manuscripts, which he had been working on at some point, ready to go over them and have a discussion about the different chapters. You know, there were people who were working on it, actually typing it up and putting things together. And he would reread and decide, well, what he liked in it and what needed to be taken out, or he would disagree with the person editing it. He always explained, if you took something out, the reason you should put it in. He would emphasize what the importance of it was, because it transmitted something in some way to people.

So, in that period leading up to his death there was always a sense of urgency that something could happen to him. He had no doubt about that and we had no doubt about it, about the possibility of death. The resulting question is about Walter's recklessness. I mean, he felt very strongly about not asking people to take risks for doing things he would not take himself. Which to me is always very strange, because usually in situations like that you know it's easier to give somebody else something to do—because it's dangerous or you're exposing yourself in certain ways. He felt very strongly that he should take his share of things in taking responsibility. And that was very unusual in those conditions, politically, when you're confronting a state.

So, we'd have meetings, and we'd have the usual arrests, the usual harassments, or police following. There were a number of times, of course, when Walter wanted to move clandestinely. He might be going to a group of people to meet somebody somewhere, whether it was in town or out of town or whatever. And that meant trying to evade observation being carried out by the police, and so you had to be hiding, you know. It was something constant. You would go in your car somewhere which is known, and you try to exchange it for somebody else's car, someone willing to lend you their vehicle and say, "Well, take it," and you go on.

Of course, a number of people put themselves at risk in terms of doing these things. Because sometimes it would go all right and you could return the vehicle and nothing happened. But there were times when you would get stopped by a patrol or someone else saw you and couldn't escape their observations. So, it was a very tense time. There was nothing that indicated anything was out of the ordinary in during that period of time. We were alerted. This was a dangerous period. Even though, I personally think that, particularly after that period, after the burning down of National Development, the lines were redrawn. It had escalated to a point where things had shifted from going in a certain direction at a certain pace, to another level. It had moved to another level.

In retrospect, how that shift and difference was dealt with, it's debatable about how we moved in that period. But there was nothing particularly different about the weeks before Walter's death.

I didn't know anything about Gregory Smith, you know. I mean, I didn't know him personally. It's only after the fact that I heard about him. This wouldn't have been unusual. I mean, the party was in a period of time where we were working in very high-security situations, so nobody would come around and say, well, we are meeting so-and-so or something. I mean, unless you were directly involved, I wouldn't have known about him or heard about him. It's not until after the fact that I knew about it.

So, I lived on Croal Street by John Street, the street that Walter was killed on. He was killed on John Street, just around by the prison. I had been out that day. I came back in the evening, it might have been about seven or eight. I lived on the top floor of this house and I was with some friends, WPA people, and I was going to get some clothes and stuff because that night I was staying by somebody's house. This was not unusual for us; for example, sometimes if one of the members was in a house by themselves, we'd go and stay with them. This person, their mother had gone away and they were in the house by themselves. So, I was to go and stay and have an extra ear and eye out in the house, so they wouldn't be by themselves. So, I was going to collect some of my stuff to go over there. When I came to the front door, I saw fresh blood on it. It was wet. I remember going back to the car. Rupert was in the car, and I can't remember everyone else who was inside there. I said, "There's fresh blood on the door and I'm not sure what that means but I want somebody to come stand at the bottom of the steps." The steps went straight up, up to the first floor, and then to the top floor. So I said, "Somebody come stand by the door and I will go upstairs." Again, we are working in a time of political insecurity, against the state. So I went up the stairs, and when I came to the top of the stairs, where it turns again, I saw Donald.[22] He was standing there.

He had just come out of the toilet and he had his shirt off and I said, "Donald, what happened?" And he didn't answer me. He stared like in a shock, and I noticed there was some blood on the side of his face. I said, "What happened?" And then he was sort of stunned and then I came up to him, and he just said, "They killed Walter." And I said, "What?" And he said, "Yes." And I said, "Where?" And he said, "It happened around the corner." I said, "Around where?" And he said, "Around John Street." So, I said, "Hold on a minute." So I was going back downstairs to tell them, and just when I was approaching the car, Andaiye and Karen[23] were coming back up the road. Because when Donald had come to the house, the two of them were home. I wasn't there.

What happened was that Walter had the bomb, a walkie-talkie, in his lap, and he was sitting next to Donald. Donald was driving the car, and Walter had the walkie-talkie [the bomb] between his legs, when the explosion went off. Donald was in shock but he had the presence of mind not to stay with the vehicle. So he ran the two blocks, two and a half blocks, then around the corner to our place and rang the bell. He told them what happened, and the two of them, Andaiye and Karen, went around the corner to look. So, when they arrived a crowd had already gathered because the explosion was loud enough for people to hear, but they were able to go up to the car and actually see Walter. But the death squad had already arrived. They recognized Andaiye and them, and they started to chase them away.

But if Donald did not have the presence of mind to leave the vehicle, they would have killed him too, because they were following him. They would have killed him, and we would not have known the link between Gregory Smith and what happened to Walter, and how he had come to meet him. So the presence of mind of Donald running away and coming toward our house is what allowed us to reconstruct the story, to really know what happened that particular night, that fatal night.

For him to recollect himself and for him to tell us exactly what happened, because if he fell into the state's hands, we were not sure what was going to happen to him. I mean, it had reached a point where they could kill him in the police station. I remember they took Donald away. Somebody just came and picked him up and decided to keep him for a couple days, and then he came forward with a statement and then he finally surrendered himself with the lawyers to the police station because the government, by then a propaganda machine, had been saying how Walter was trying to blow up the jail to let prisoners out.

There was a mobile police station around the prison, and they had moved that station away. When you asked people if they noticed things, it was only when the story was reconstructed that people began to notice things. The mobile police station was there partly because prisoners, as they still do it to now, were escaping over the walls every now and then. And so, they had that station. But it had been removed that same night. Earlier they took that mobile police station away without any explanation. People in the road noticed it, wondered why they were suddenly, in the night, moving the station.

Walter was supposed to be there, correct. Gregory Smith had given Walter instructions to stop by the prison to test if those zinc sheets that covered the prison would affect the communication equipment.[24] But Walter had gone another block away. He decided not to stop there because it would've been, I suppose, unusual for them to have stopped and parked outside the prison. Nobody parked outside on that side of the road. And he had decided to go a block down the road.

So, we decided not to stay at the same house. We went on to another house, and a lot of friends came to that house to stay. Of course, everybody was in total shock, and this was nighttime. You can't be walking on the streets, and you can't be outside because you know that if they organized this, then the whole security apparatus is on full alert. And you know you can't afford to be caught outside, or else anything could happen. And so the next day we began to start working and finding out information and reconstructing exactly what had happened. And as each day went by, we were able to, piece by piece, add something more onto it, in terms of finding out how it happened. I remember going that same night with Malcolm Rodrigues, who was a Jesuit priest and who had been a friend of Walter's and had been involved in WPA, to look for Pat [Walter's wife] to tell her. Pat had been with the children at St. Rose's High School. There was a concert or something, and we had to go and tell her about this incident that happened. Malcolm went upstairs and went to look for her to bring her and tell her. We took her home. She had the two little girls with her, Asha and Kanini. They were small at that time, of course, and it was really just so heartbreaking.

We weren't there when they came, but the police actually came and searched the house too. Which, to me, is also a level of cruelty, whatever one wants to say about Burnham and that regime. That they would have known that they had killed this man, but his wife, you know what I mean? Why would you send police to search their house, to go through, to add this even more to her grief and to her burden, stuff like that? There was a certain cruelty about it. But I suppose it's what Walter represented too. One of the things I've heard PNC people say, up to now, is how angry they were about how Walter spoke about Burnham in that denigrating way, calling him King Kong and talking about him having the opposite of the Midas touch[25] and stuff like that. They personally felt angry about those things. So, if you read about Burnham's "personal" thing, about what his own sister wrote about him, these things were not unusual.[26] He took things personally, in that personal way. He would not forget. Fifteen, twenty years after, he would remember what you did to him.

This thing could escalate. We might be having an armed confrontation with the state, and therefore we should prepare ourselves, arm ourselves. Yet we had no capacity to do anything with it. We were still in the process of gathering as much as we could. We didn't have access to steal things—you know, you could get a gun here, you could get a gun there, you could get someone to smuggle it in from here or whatever. We didn't have like large truckloads or anything coming in.

Nobody was helping us; no state was helping us or anything like that. We just decided that we were going to prepare ourselves in terms of what we thought might be an inevitable struggle against the state's response. I mean we were not playing by any sort of state rules and then the state will step back and say, well, we are going to wait until you reach your capacity and we feel like you're at the tipping point and then we will deal with you. We are dealing with a state that is a dictatorship, and it's a police state, and they will respond and we also understood that too.

People say how Walter had been reckless. Who is not? I mean, Martin Luther King could be considered reckless. I mean, if you put people out there they may be nonviolent; but it doesn't mean that people didn't get killed, that people were not beaten. Anytime you challenge a state, these things are going to happen. There is no way you can protect everybody or anybody, or else it's best you don't struggle. I mean, whether you are in a slave situation or people are in slavery, you know they plan to get away or to overthrow the master, try to take over the estate. Each one is fraught with danger. It's either you submit or you continue in a capacity that you just don't do anything.

I've heard somebody, an intellectual person, who was there at Walter's anniversary,[27] raise this question that Walter was reckless in some terms, and you ask, "Reckless how? In what way do you consider him reckless?" When you are fighting against a police state, the minute that you begin to fight against it you are putting yourself in danger and you're also putting the people you lead or the people that join you, you're putting them in danger. It is an understanding you have that once you enter this field, you may not come out of it alive, or you'll be in jail for the rest of your life or tortured.

Those black people who took part in that struggle here in the United States—I have such respect for them. You know, Martin has a line in one of his poems that says, "You rude people of the world, don't you think I know that hate is shouted and love is stuttered." I love you, but hate, it's easier to go to that side, and it's easier to go to the dark side. It's easier to embrace it, that part where you say you will not do the things. And people, I think, still do not respect, in particular black people, what it took for King to take that position and for the people who followed him to take that position.

Even though Walter had the experience of working in Africa— and we've all read historic facts about struggles, whether it is Cuba or Algeria or one of those places, and you know what happens— when you're actually living it, having to deal with it, I think you make mistakes. Walter was a young person too. He was thirty-eight. We all, I think, felt there was a certain arrogance. Somehow when you say those things it seems people use it who want to criticize us, and say, well there you know, they see it. But there was a feeling of what we were struggling for with this higher idea. I mean, we were young in terms of twenties, thirties, and even though we knew the danger we still did not grasp things in a real fundamental way. We didn't understand. Burnham. I mean we used to make jokes about him, but you know Burnham is not a stupid man; he is a clever man.

Of all the Caribbean politicians, even the ones of his generation like Manley and Barrow[28] and stuff like that, he was a worthy adversary. He was a worthy person to fight against, because he thought things through. For instance, he had the regular standing army. He had the National Service. He had the paramilitary People's Militia. His thing was looking at those African countries where the army decides, "Well, why are we holding power for you when we could hold it ourselves?" So his thing is that he created this thing over here, and this thing over there, so if you get out of place he's going to bring this one over here to counter you.

Last year, I was reading a review for a book on Stalin, about people who had worked around him and how contemptuous he had become of them. When I read this thing I said this is just like Burnham. He brought all these people around him who would agree with whatever he said. It reaches a point, when you do that, that people can tell you the sky is green. And you can't change them because Comrade Leader said the sky was green. But it really is blue, you know, but you can't convince them otherwise.

A friend of mine who was an officer in the National Service said that he was talking to Burnham in his office and Burnham was complaining about a permanent secretary from one of the ministries. He said look at this, and he calls him and he puts on the speakerphone and the man said, "Comrade, we don't hear from you, you don't give instructions anymore about what to do, I didn't hear from you for a long time." So now Burnham gave him this job and put him in this position, but this man doesn't have a capacity to make judgments on his own about how to run the state. And so you have this yes-man, and then this department you have or this government you're

running is collapsing around you, because he doesn't have the capacity to make the decisions. It frustrated Burnham because everything
was collapsing around him because he put people in positions they
can't handle, that don't know how to do things. You know, Guyana
is one of the few places, or the only place in the Caribbean, that,
after the end of that period, had the capacity to make something
real out of it. We had so many well-trained people, so many well-
trained people. It's only because Burnham came with this thing that
you have to be loyal to the party and to him, and it began to move
people away. People began migrating. People would just do things,
you know, in this job you thieving all you can because the job can
end anytime.

They opened a textile mill. Why don't they have those students
at the school who are interested in textile, let them come here, let
them come once a week. During the holidays, let them do appren-
ticeships in the thing, give them a stipend. You know, if you pay
them to be off the street or to be something they will. Let them
come in and learn the process of it. You'll be amazed sometimes,
some of those students I am teaching could come up with better
ideas or designs than I do.[29] And I recognize that sometimes you
can tap into a talent that is there naturally. Someone can take this
stuff to the market and sell it. For example, you do ten yards of a
piece of cloth, go by the market, and sell it to the public at a rea-
sonable price. You know people will come and say, I like this, and
they'll buy it. Then you'll see how well they are responding to this
floral or this particular design. I gave this whole idea to them, they
refused to take it.

A lot of the time, they brought people back to Guyana; they were
sending people to study art in Cuba; there were people who were
going to Europe, stuff like that. They were coming back home during the summer to do nothing. That's how it was. I said why don't
they do stuff in art? In the summer let's use Bishops' or QC[30] as an
art place and invite people from the public. It doesn't matter if they
know about art. I mean, everyone does art in school at one point. We
could provide newsprint paper, provide the simple things. We could

teach them how to do sketches, to do a little ceramics and stuff like that and get the stuff fired and so on. It would be a good introduction for these people that want to go into teaching or are just going with the thing. But the public also becomes more aware of art, and you could have an exhibition at the end. I went to the Ministry of Culture to propose the idea to the permanent secretary. She said an idea like that can't come from somebody like you; it has to come out of the ministry. You know, this got me so angry. I said, "There is no wonder we will always remain an underdeveloped country because of the stupid decisions that ya'll make."

I went back to Guyana for the scholarship. What happened is that my father was paying for my school and then Burnham intervened. I've known Burnham since I was a little boy. He'd been a friend of the family. My sister's father is Dr. Frank Williams, and he was Burnham's personal physician. So when he heard that it was my last year, he said that the government was flush with money from the sugar industry, and they were giving scholarships to all these mostly black and regular class people. And I said yes, you know. They said they were going to pay for the last year of school. It's not that we, my family, didn't have money to pay for me. I had no objections to it because I wanted to come back. I agreed with the government that you have to do four or five years of National Service. I saw nothing wrong with that, you know, that the state pays for you. The thing about it is that Burnham and the PNC are not the people that provide that money for you; it's just channeled through them. The wealth of Guyana is produced through sugar workers, bauxite workers, gold diggers, whose children would most likely not see any of that money or wealth. So I felt, why not? If I come back and give five years, ten years, for the rest of my life, I will want to give back, in service toward this country. I had no objections to doing that. So I said, "Yes I'll take it."

So, when I came back home I actually got a job. They didn't want to give me a job at the art school, but Dennis Williams, who was the principal of the art school, who I knew personally, said, "Come," and he hired me. He sent me to the minister of culture saying, "I've hired

Abbyssinian." They didn't hire me in an official capacity. They didn't make me sign any documents, because by that time they knew that I was involved in WPA. Eventually it came to a point where they told me I could no longer work there; they didn't fire me, but they told me I couldn't come back in the school anymore and I wasn't allowed to teach there anymore because of my involvement in WPA.

So I stopped teaching at the school. Even though you have all these people who might not have the same political views as you but who are interested. You know how many people out of that period never came back to Guyana. Yeah, they never went back. They were not interested in returning once they got the education, they stayed outside. Some of them paid back the money, or their parents were forced to pay it back. But some of them never paid it back. I felt, because of my political awareness, that this money was really coming from a set of people who created the wealth of this country. And I have a right in terms of taking their money. I felt strongly about growing up in a Third World country. I think we could make ourselves into something. I didn't think we could be a First World country. I didn't think it could be like here in the States or anything like that, but we could make ourselves into a viable something. It's one of my angers about things, that up to now Guyana is in that state, you know, because of where we started on that path from that time.

4—Dr. Brenda Do Harris

I returned to Guyana in December 1973. I worked at the Ministry of Information for about a year. Then in 1975, I went to Bishops' High School where I started teaching. When I went back home, I really was not interested in getting involved in anything beyond myself and my friends. But the situation, as I saw it gradually evolving, required some kind of participation.

My brother, who was an officer in the Guyana National Service,[1] had told me there were people in the National Service who had been abused. He started documenting some of these instances of abuse. During this time I met Eusi Kwayana.[2] Given the political climate, we did not feel comfortable going to people in established areas of authority. Somebody suggested Eusi Kwayana. We told him about it, and he became involved immediately. I think I can count my own involvement from that period, because he was an immense source of example for me as a person who was involved in the movement for working people. During that time I helped him to put together an article for publication in the *Contact*[3] newspaper that had to do with conditions in the National Service.

I also was an analyst at Radio Demerara. I would come on the air in the mornings, and I began talking about some of the inequities that I saw in the treatment of people in the country and particularly political victimizations. Many of my observations on air often went counter to what the government thought should be put out there. After a while people stopped talking to you because it became very dangerous for them to be seen associating with you if one was considered anti-government. I think I did it because I was educated in the United States at the tertiary level and after living here and seeing that people were, more or less open—and I say more or less—in their observations about what was going on, I went home and I did it. But it carried a certain price.

As time went on, I realized that I associated mostly with the Working People's Alliance, and I found myself drawn into it. Eusi was an indefatigable advocate for working people and the cases we brought to him. I realized that the Working People's Alliance was an association I needed to join.

It's about this time I met Walter Rodney. Now, sometimes I look back on it and think that the six years I spent in Guyana were, in a sense, detrimental to my professional development. But then, when I really review it, I have to say absolutely no. Because I grew in terms of my association with the people in the WPA: people like Walter Rodney, Bonita Harris, Andaiye, Ohene Koama, now dead, also assassinated. I found that I grew politically, that there were things I learned that set me apart from others over here [in the United States] and with whom I had graduated and who had not gone through some of these experiences.

My last encounter with Walter is the thing that causes me the most guilt, and it's the thing, too, that makes me so silent about affairs dealing with Guyana—silent, now thirty years later.

I remember I was preparing to leave the country when I saw him last. I was about to return to New York, to Brooklyn, where my mother lived. I saw him on Main Street. He was walking alone. And when I saw him, I slowed down. Of course, he was alone because everybody knew he was Walter Rodney and many people were afraid to associate with you publicly if you were with the opposition. I slowed, and we spoke. He said to me, "I need to have a car. I need to borrow your car. Can I meet you at your home later on and pick it up?" I told him I would be home at 2:30. I went to the BWIA [airlines] office, and it was packed with people all trying to get out. I was held up and did not get home until 3:15. When I got home, my next-door neighbor said to me, "God, yuh know wuh, Walter Rodney was sittin' down on yuh backstep waitin' fuh yuh to come home. He wait one whole hour, a whole hour duh man sid down and wait. He miss yuh. He miss yuh." I went to his house afterward. But he was not there.

When I heard that he had been destroyed, I was in Brooklyn. I felt really devastated. I was devastated because the last time I saw him, he had asked me to do something for him, and I was not able to do it.

Before this, I had gotten involved in the trade union movement. The Public Service Union [PSU] was the country's largest trade union and at that time, as I recall, the most vibrant. The president was Norman Semple, who was a kind of protégé of the government. But I came on with many analyses talking about the deficiencies of the leadership of the PSU. I kind of talked myself into being asked to run for the presidency of the union. This was at a time when women were not often in leadership, and I was in many organizations in which I was the only woman. That did not make me feel very comfortable. But it was something I thought I had to do. One of the people in the WPA came to me and asked if I would be their candidate in the election. I thought about it and decided I would do it. But it turned out to be one of the most frightening periods of my life in terms of government harassment: seeing yourself being followed when you left home, and so on.

At the same time, my brother, who lived with me—he and his wife, we all shared a house together—had just had a baby. That baby is now twenty-something. At the time she was just three months old, and I kept thinking that this was not a good situation. It was a time when police can come into your house, plant weapons, take you away, and so on. They had done that with Bonita Bone. We knew that Walter was hiding and very often not staying in the same house every night. So it was a very unsettling situation and not the kind of thing you wanted to involve a baby in. That made me a bit uncomfortable. But then, my brother himself joined the WPA. We both lost our jobs as a result.

I was transferred to Port Kaituma, which is near Jonestown. He was transferred to a place named Konashen. He had worked in the public service for about eighteen years. He was a senior civil servant. But because he was seen at some meeting handing out flyers for the WPA, he was dismissed and sent to Konashen. I was terrified of going to a place named Jonestown. Having been sent by a government that I thought was very violent. So I had to leave Guyana. I had to leave in order to support myself.

I am still looking back on it, thirty years later, riddled with guilt about leaving, because there were others who stayed. I keep coming back to my old school friend, Bonita Harris: a woman with a lot of spirit who stayed and continued the fight. She and Andiaye and Karen DeSouza, and I am by no means mentioning everyone who was engaged in that battle. I think those people need to forgive me if I left them out. But life in Guyana at the time was frightening beyond measure if you were involved in political activities.

When I look back on it now, I think of this as a retrospective. I am sixty-one now. I don't care who knows it. I am not sure, because I did a lot of this when I was thirty, and at thirty you think of yourself as invincible and that life will continue and never end. Looking back now, I wonder if I would have taken some of those risks that I did. But always I was guided, and it's the same reason why I write now, by a principle that this was my country. This is the country in which my father had taken me to political meetings when I was ten years old and drilled me in the political system. He had us reading the newspapers. He was a kind of nut in this respect. He had us reading political articles and questioned us on it later on. I think this helped to keep me involved as an adult. But I treasure the experience.

I was not a close associate of Walter. I wouldn't say, like other people, that he and I "used to hang." We didn't. But I met him on various occasions, at political meetings, and he was always very encouraging toward me and the analysis I did. He always called me "Sister" and was always loving in his approaches, always gentle and loving. I think Guyana lost a good deal when he went. I am not sure the country will ever get that back. That is the extent of my desolation over what has transpired since. I don't think we will get it back. We will strive for it. But I have a feeling of hopelessness sometimes when I look at the situation today.

One of the interesting things is that I have come across people, some in my own family, who were devoted members of the PNC, who have said to me, "Well yuh see wuh ya'll do. Dis is wuh ya'll gih we." Meaning, of course, the present government and all its excesses. But even with the present government, at the beginning things could have been done in such a way that it did not have to come to this. I think Guyana has been destroyed by racial division. We are at a point where it is so sad that people we can't see past differences in race. I think ultimately we may go the way of a Rwanda if that situation doesn't change, or Sri Lanka if the situation doesn't improve.

5—Robert Hill

There were never flyers. There was nothing ever announced. Rastafarians evolved this ritual practice that Walter adapted to. And it basically consists of Rastas sitting around a campfire, lighting a pipe, singing praises to his majesty, reciting prayers, but the thing that keeps fueling it and driving it are reasonings. A topic will emerge and different individuals will approach it and start to debate it, and then there will be prayers and more pipe smoking. The lighting of the pipe is very important because of the evocations they make in the process of lighting the pipe. And when the pipe is passed, it can only be passed in the left hand going that way. That film—something about the debt—had some tremendous footage of Rastafarian reasonings.[1]

When Walter came to Jamaica, he started speaking on the campus of the University of the West Indies. But there was a small Rastafarian contingent. Anything about Africa has instant appeal to Rastafarians, and so when they heard about this young brother who had lived in Africa, taught about Africa, they immediately established contact on the campus with Walter. But apart from Walter's public lectures on Black Power on the campus, his connection with the Rastafarian community was off-campus. And this is the thing that set off the alarms bells with the government, because as word began to spread that Walter was meeting with people in their own locals, the idea that an intellectual was leaving the campus and going down into the inner-city and meeting wherever people wanted to meet with him—this had never been done before.. That set off alarm bells.

And then as these groundations[2] developed, on a Sunday morning there could be 200 to 300 people just sitting around and Walter speaking, talking to them. And, of course, he never talked down to them. He talked perfectly normal, in a way that anybody could understand. Walter said he learned from them more than they learned from him because he discovered that they had their own remarkable pedagogy for developing ideas about their reality. So, this was a phenomenon to see in action.

Walter and I left in October of 1968 to attend the Black Writers' Congress in Montreal, and we presented a paper on the Jamaican situation because we knew the situation was developing, was becoming critical in Jamaica. And that paper forms the preface to the book *Groundings with My Brothers*.[3] Walter spoke at the Congress and then left to go back, and at this time Walter's wife was probably six, seven months pregnant. I stayed in Canada. I had planned to spend a few days extra in Montreal because my brother was there. My plan was then to go from Montreal to Toronto. When Walter landed in Jamaica, the government declared him a prohibited immigrant. So, since he was deported, wasn't allowed to land, he was returned to Montreal, and the following day the university's students took to the streets and a popular protest developed.[4] And I think that October 1968 really constitutes a political divide in the modern history of the Caribbean, because it not only developed a protest movement in Jamaica but throughout the Caribbean, Trinidad, Guyana, Grenada, Antigua. It's as if what took place in Jamaica just like lit a spark, and that the modern political history of the Caribbean can be defined as before October 1968 and after October 1968. That was how important Walter was.

Walter spent a few days with us in Canada. I left Walter there, and he asked me to take a letter to Pat.[5] When I got back, when I landed in Jamaica, it was a Sunday evening. And I felt before even going to see my own family that I wanted to take the letter to Pat because I knew how worried she must be. I recall my mother meeting me at the airport, and we drove straight to the campus and it was ringed by soldiers and police with machine guns aimed at the entrance. And no students, no one was allowed on or off the campus, and I argued and insisted that I should be admitted. I was a student. I had every right to go to the university and I took the letter.

But see, Pat had been in the march with the students, from the campus heading down toward Kingston, and the police had tried to head it off at the major junction when you leave the campus. They tried to stop it with tear gas. Pat took a lot of tear gas, and in the stampede she got buffeted around. So, there was a question about whether she might miscarry. The doctors had asked that she be kept in bed and monitored who could come and see her. I wasn't allowed to actually go into the room. I think they said she was resting, but I left the letter with someone I knew who was taking care of her.

She was being cared for by the warden of Mary Seacole Hall. That woman was a Guyanese, actually, and is, well, I hesitate to say where she is now. She was in charge of the UN Conference on Women, the first UN conference on women. She played a very important role at the United Nations, and she's a very well-known Caribbean historian. I don't know if she's alive. I'm kind of hesitating, her name will come back to me, but her father was the great West Indian writer Eric Walrond,[6] who was Guyanese. Anyway she was the warden,[7] and Pat, after the march, was taken to Mary Seacole Hall and was being looked after there. It was kind of touch and go. They were worried about whether she would have a miscarriage, and at that late term a miscarriage would have been very very tricky.

So I did see Walter and felt his impact both before we left Jamaica and after. After I returned and he had been deported I went to Atlanta, in the spring of 1970. Walter came to speak at the AHSA, that is, the African Heritage Studies Association, at their first national and international conference held at Howard University's Crampton Auditorium. Walter came from Tanzania to speak. Then we invited him. That would have been around, sort of like, June of 1970. From there he came to visit the Institute of the Black World[8] where I was also visiting and that's where he fell ill. And no doctors there could figure out what was wrong with him. He was just getting progressively weaker and weaker and running a very high temperature. And it was somebody from the CDC in Atlanta, I believe, who finally said it's malaria. See, most doctors today have never seen malaria and therefore if someone is ill with it, they don't know what it is. So, somebody from the CDC did a test and said it's malaria, but before that Walter's situation was becoming pretty desperate, and so we sent a ticket for Pat and the kids to come over.

The last time I saw Walter was probably 1980. We arranged for him to give a lecture at UCLA, and I'd also arranged for him to speak at the University of California, Santa Barbara. I remember we left the campus at UCLA, must've been like ten in the morning because Santa Barbara is a little over two hours' drive away. We were to get there, have lunch, and then he was going to give the lecture. We were driving up Sepulveda Boulevard, and I said, "You know, Walter, we are definitely interested and would like you to come back next year now that we have a little bit of lead time." Because that particular visit was arranged at very short notice, I thought maybe we could spend part of the time on the drive to Santa Barbara talking about the logistics for next year. And he said to me, "I won't be here next year." And I said, "Why? Why wouldn't you, next year, just like we did this year?" He said, "I won't be here next year." I said, "Wait a minute, Walter. What are you talking about?" He said, "Just what I told you. I won't be here." And I remember saying, "Maybe you're being a little morbid." Somehow he knew: some sign, some premonition. But, you know, he said it so matter-of-factly; it wasn't said with any dread. It was just, "You are asking me to talk about logistics of next year, but I won't be here, so what's the point?" And he was assassinated, and that was my last meeting with him.

It was a Friday night and I had gone home. It was about eight o'clock. I remember it was dark outside. I went into my house and got a telephone call from Bill Strickland,[9] and he said to me, "Are you sitting down?" And I said, "No, I just walked in the house." And he said, "Well, you need to sit down," and then he said, "I just heard the news, Walter has been assassinated."

We didn't have much information, but he had heard. And he and I are very close friends. So, I figured I must've been one of the first people he called. We had all been together at the Institute in Atlanta. So, we had shared that experience and then Walter came back to Atlanta, once or twice, to visit. I would arrange to be there when Walter was visiting. So, Atlanta was important for Walter in the same way that Atlanta is significant for Pat today.

6—Amiri Baraka

When I met Walter, he was in Tanzania. He had just gotten sick, and he was in the hospital in Dar es Salaam. I talked to him a couple times there, before I left. That was the first time I met him, in Dar es Salaam. But I had known his writing, and I had heard about him from the people and the general kind of Pan-Africanist groups, and when I got to Tanzania, one of my closest friends there, Muhammad Babu,[1] talked about Walter a lot. So I think we had a kind of cordiality among us based on what we thought—our ideological development, you see.

I went to Tanzania three times, and probably the last time was the Sixth Pan-African Congress.[2] But now, it was clear to me that people who had been nationalists were sort of trying to find more solid ground as far as nationalism was concerned, because it was going into the whole cultural nationalist thing then and getting involved in a lot of atavism and worship of the past, and so forth and so on.

So there, Rodney was similar to Cabral[3] in that he had a more materialist approach to the whole *business* of struggle. That's what attracted me to him. One of the things Walter always said that was important to me was: "We cannot let racism and white supremacy deprive us of the most important things white people have said." He was talking about Marxism, and I thought it was very important at the time to hear that, because that was clearly right. I mean, you couldn't let backward racists make it impossible for you to understand scientific socialism. I mean, there are still a lot of black people around today, that I could name, that still need to heed that advice and who are still so, what could you call it, just so blitzed, intellectually, by racism that they can't deal with the question of scientific socialism. That's still very clear and very true.

What's important about Tanzania is, even now, Nyerere talking about Ujamaa as some kind of African socialism. Ujamaa, the question of socialism, was on the table. The question is, how are you going to deal with it? Plus, as you began to talk to the people who were actually involved in the African liberation movement, they were all socialists. I mean, except for people like in UNITA[4] or some right-wing group. Most of those people, when you talk about MPLA[5] or TANU,[6] they were talking about socialism. FRELIMO,[7] ANC[8]—they were talking about socialism. So the question was of how you embrace that, particularly in the West, the United States and the Caribbean. How do you embrace that? And that's what made that important.

That period between let's say 1968, the whole Black Power thing coming in, and then what we did in the whole Gary Convention,[9]1972, and in 1970 the Congress of African People[10] meeting in Atlanta, where there were people from the African liberation movements present—that was saying we can. The Black Panthers had their constitutional convention in Philadelphia. They had 4,000; we had 2,000 in Atlanta. It was like a great many black people were discussing not just the liberation of the United States but the liberation of African people.

So in 1972 you had the Gary Convention, trying to deal with the power in the United States. How do we seize power in the United States? And then the same year, a couple months later, you had the African Liberation Support Committee and in that committee they began to wage this two-line struggle. That was where the struggle was, really, attempting to connect with Africa. You had people like

Owusu Sadaukai,[11] Carmichael,[12] who'd gone to Africa and come back, and all the different groups. That was when the struggle heated up, about which way, which direction it would go. In fact, that was the conference, 1974, in which the black liberation movement participated. Those years, 1970 on, it was really intensified about socialism or Black Nationalism. And Rodney was an important thinker there because he was definitely a socialist and was saying, just like Cabral, that we have to learn from everybody.

So, that was very important. It's funny. The United States particularly is funny because even today with the Obama thing, which is to me a continuation of the civil rights movement, black liberation, there is still the same struggle. There are still people who refuse to understand that the key question is the struggle for power and scientific socialism. They still refuse. I don't know whether they want to take it all the way back to this kind of cultural nationalism stuff. You got a conference down in Miami coming up in a week or so [2009] where they're talking the same stuff they were talking forty years ago. Or where you have these people that think of themselves as the black left, not Marxist-Leninist, but the black left, and who seem to be nationalist influenced.

In 1967 all the rebellions happened. Detroit[13] and Newark[14] exploded. In 1965 it was Watts,[15] you understand: Malcolm's murder. In 1956 the Montgomery bus boycott[16] was successfully ended. But at the same time, that's when they blew up Dr. King's house in Montgomery. The black people showed up with the rifles and said, "What should we do, Dr. King?" and he said, "If any blood be shed let it be ours." There was a whole generation of us who did not accept that. I mean we certainly loved Dr. King and supported Dr. King, but the idea that somehow if any bleeding was going down we were going to have to do the bleeding—we didn't accept that.

That's when Malcolm X appeared, and Malcolm said you treat people like they treat you. If they treat you with respect, you treat them with respect. If they put their hands on you, you send them to the cemetery. It was a whole generation of us excited by that. Yes, you did have the right to self-defense, you know. All those things were coming together, and like I said, 1967—those rebellions and the Black Power Conference in Newark in 1967.[17] I was just coming out of prison. And then, 1968, you have Carmichael and King on the road and that's when they start shouting "Black Power!" So you have all of that coming together. I mean, the period from the late 1950s through into the 1970s was really very intense, very intense. And for struggle, here, it was because of the Black Power conference and then the conference for African people and then the Panther constitutional conference[18] and the Gary convention and the African Liberation Support Committee. All those things were booom! booom! booom! That was a generation really trying to find its way and that never stopped actually. It just happened more sporadically, because Nixon came on the scene.

What Nixon did is divide the movement. He put out the idea of black capitalism. Then, J. Edgar[19] killed the militants at the same time. You see, it was really the way of dealing with it. He cooled out one whole sector of the movement and divided it by talking about black capitalism. And so, there were some people who went for that, the idea. And then the other groups, of course, they were then harassed and murdered and locked up, some still in prison all these years. But that, the legacy of that, went through the movement, see. So that on the black capitalism side, you could finally get Condoleezza Rice[20] and a Powell.[21] You could generate these CEOs, at Time Warner,[22] all those things. I mean, you could generate that and you could actually cool out the national movement to a certain extent.

On the other side, there was some kind of activity in town, the electoral thing. Jesse Jackson,[23] certainly that was important. There was a lot of confusion, too, because the people who were the most militant were killed and then, you remember, you lost Malcolm X, Martin Luther King, a little while later Carmichael died; Rap Brown is in prison for life. The whole confusion with the Nation of Islam, in terms of, some people still holding them responsible for Malcolm's murder and Farrakhan's role. So it's been very confusing to a certain extent since then. But see, the dynamic of that is what, even today, creates an Obama: that's still the force of the people. They haven't stopped.

Actually, the Obama thing is what united them on a higher level. Ninety-eight percent of 45 million people, the Afro-American people, voted for him. Because without the Afro-American, and the Latinos to some extent, Obama wouldn't be the president. But the question that Rodney and I and some other people were arguing about nationalism and socialism, still remains very key. As a matter fact, I'm writing an essay, my last essay of the set, maybe not the last one. But I wrote about six or seven essays on Obama since 2007, early in 2007, and the one now [2008] to sum it up just before the inauguration: where we are. We are still fighting with some people who want to say Obama's election is just to preserve capitalism, and so forth and so on. I mean, to be that simple-minded. Some of these nationalists that want to call themselves the black left believe that anarchism or Trotskyism makes them militant. You know what I mean? And it doesn't. You couldn't say that about when we were getting killed to integrate bathrooms and lunch counters. We were going to jail to integrate bus terminals. Do they think that Obama's presidency is less significant? You know what I mean? It's just too crazy, and you have to see things as they actually are and see that things proceed in stages, step by step, and you have to be able to understand at what stage you're at and then seize the next level to go forward.

There is no such thing as a sweeping revolution. This is not nineteenth-century Russia or twentieth-century China. This is the twenty-first century in the most advanced capitalist country in the world.

So, unless you approach it that way, then you're always on the margins making quotes. But the actuality of power, which is what revolution is supposed to be, to seize power, never comes to pass. So there are people who still maintain this kind of soggy nationalism, who refuse to embrace the whole question of scientific socialism. What do we do to transform this country into a socialist country? What do we do? You don't think that the election of Obama makes us a step closer? The right does. They know that. I mean, a fool in Michigan, on the day after the election, is standing on a corner in a

Klan uniform, a Republican delegate, who, when they ask him, says that "Obama is an Islamic communist, a black Islamic communist." I mean, he needs to die three times.

But it's still that kind of murky question of are you a nationalist or are you a socialist? And I think that is something we still have to thrash out here, in the twenty-first century. We're still going to have to thrash that and fight that and get some clarity on it and make demands of people in terms of clarification of the ideology.

You see, King and Malcolm X are both representatives of the African American people, different ideological aspects of them, but they killed them both. How much greater would it have been if we had been in one party and we could've argued those things endlessly inside that. You understand. The same thing with Marcus Garvey and W. E. B. Du Bois—they exiled both of them. Wherever you thought you were standing in that, you have to see that it's the whole thing that's offensive to the oppressors, not this aspect or that aspect, but the whole thing. And until you can find a way to unify that whole, like I mean 98 percent of people, of black people, voted for Obama, that's the kind of unity we're going to need to get rid of the rest of this. And I think that that's why, right now, the main push has to be to get a big united front for a democratic coalition and government and to get rid of the legacy of racism and white supremacy and also to end the complete domination of monopoly capital over the people's needs.

I mean, if we give a trillion or two trillion dollars to those people, then I don't want oversight over those banks, I want to own those banks. See, I don't want to give 250 billion dollars to the auto industry and say we have oversight over it. If we give them 250 billion, we got to own it: the United States auto companies. You know what I'm saying? All those mortgages should be paid to the government. Those banks should not be allowed to be out there like that, you understand? If you want private enterprise, then deal with it privately. You can't tell me about the market system and free enterprise and then you going to come to me with your tin cup for two trillion dollars. I'm not making twenty million dollars a year. There was some hearing on television the other day. The guys from Lehman Brothers, bankrupt company, he left with 580 million dollars. So, then, he argues with the guy who questioned him, "That's not accurate, those figures are not accurate." Well, how much did you leave with? He goes, "380 million dollars." So, I mean, if you could play with that kind of money, beautiful, do that. But then when you stub your toe, don't come to me. See, who has millions of starving people, unemployed people, to deal with and take care of? You understand what I'm saying? Those are the things I think this Obama thing [is connected to] and why we have to finally connect this nationalism and socialism that these people are talking about, these divisions, because now we have to unify the majority of people into a position: black ones and white ones to end white supremacy, end racism, pass some laws against it.

You understand, we are at that point right now, when Obama talks about a post-racial coalition we should see that. When the people are angry about these monopolists getting two trillion dollars, we should seize on that. Those points are clearer in people's minds. I don't mean leftist or revolutionist. The people now understand that it is time to get rid of racism. It's time to get these people off our backs, you see. And if there is any leadership, among the people that are so-called revolutionary, they should be trying to fight for the leadership of that rather than be sitting on the side criticizing Obama before he even gets into office. It's incredible, incredible.

Like this whole thing about Rahm Emanuel as the Chief of Staff, the Jewish dude, I thought it was a great thing. Because who do these people think they're going to be criticizing? They already are calling the president Hussein. You know what I mean? And that he's Muslim and all kind of stuff. Who better to get to sit at your door than a pugilistic Jew who is a close friend of his? I mean, you got to understand politics, man. It's not a glee club or a tea party. You've got to use the weapons that you can think up, and he's been right so far. The decision not to take public funds, that was correct because it didn't limit him in his monies.[24] His decision to use the Biden thing and then to put Hillary and them outside of the inner circle, that was correct. So we'll see.

But, with Rodney that's just part of the kind of intellectual legacy of the Pan-Africanist movement. I mean, when you have people like C. L. R. James and Rodney and Carmichael, as well as Malcolm and people like that, you have to see that as the intellectual legacy that you can borrow and use anytime you want to.

Well, that's what I'm saying; the whole Pan-Africanist struggle in essence is for what—self-determination, equal rights. Wherever in the world, it's the same thing. The so-called focus of any revolutionary is the seizure of power. Not to see Obama related to that is not to understand the movement. You see, to have a black dude as the president of the United States is important. How we utilize that, that's on you. That's on us. But he obviously knows what he's doing. The question is, do we know what we are doing?

And I wish Walter Rodney was alive so he could dig this. I know it would crack him up, you know. Very funny. Stokely, I know, he would laugh and laugh. Because, ultimately, what it is, what these people don't understand is that that boy is smart. And they don't know about black people. There are a million of us around this planet who are as smart as Obama and who know exactly what this is and what needs to be done to it. Walter Rodney's thing about "How Europe Underdeveloped Africa" is a textbook, a primer to learning about colonialism and international oppression. And so, we have to see from that how monopoly capitalism underdevelops the Afro-American community, the Latino community, and the Caribbean community, and now, the United States is multinational, multicultural. There are so many Puerto Ricans, Dominicans, Ecuadorians, Jamaicans, and Haitians in this town, in New York, it's incredible. You can't be anywhere, at least in the Northeast where I live, that's not definitely multinational, multicultural. And that's part of the weight we bring to this now. It's not just us anymore. It's not just black Americans anymore. All these people are exploited, you see.

7—Leith Mullings

I went to Tanzania in 1970, and I was there from May to about the beginning of November. I was a graduate student at the time. 1970 was a very tumultuous time. The Vietnam War was on. In the United States protesting students from Kent State and JacksonState universities had been killed protesting the Vietnam War. In Tanzania, anti-colonial movements were in the midst of their most important activity. So, in Dar es Salaam,[1] you could meet freedom fighters from the Caribbean, from all over Africa, and from the United States. So, it was a very exciting place to be.

The Tanzanian government offered asylum to liberation movements that were illegal or banned in their own countries. President Julius Nyerere,[2] the first president of Tanzania, was attempting to build a different kind of society called Ujamaa, meaning African socialism, where there was more equal distribution of resources. This was a tremendously different project, and there was a great deal of excitement. So people, scholars, flocked there from all over the world to try to participate in this new endeavor, and Walter Rodney was really the center of a large group of intellectuals who were very much involved with the building of society.

The Black Power tendency had a current that was very Pan-Africanist. It was also the case that there were a fair number of people who were on the run from the U.S. government, and you could run into some of them in Tanzania where they were given refuge. But I would say that Pan-Africanism certainly had a long history in the United States, and it comes out in the Black Power movement, as well as inother directions and paradigms.

I was a teaching assistant at the University of Dar es Salaam, and I met Walter because most of the faculty knew each other. It was very exciting to meet Walter. Walter was really a star at the university. He was really a quick thinker and a prolific writer. People just milled around him, basically. You couldn't be there and not know Walter Rodney.

He and Pat would invite us to their house to socialize. I was looking in my diary in preparation for this interview and I found an entry for"Rodney Party." So people were not only doing a lot of work and thinking hard, they were also, as African-descended people all over the world, living life to its fullest whenever possible. By "Rodney Party," I did not mean the WPA. This party began at 9:30 at night.

He was a tremendously warm person and very unassuming. He was certainly very, very in tune with people of African descent in various liberation movements, from the United States, certainly the Caribbean, and from Africa as well. He was easy to talk to and he was funny, a real pleasure to be around.

One of the interesting things about the university at that time is that it was not an ivory tower situation. The university students and the university faculty were very involved in thinking about the direction of the country. For example, a debate was scheduled on the question of tourism. One of the possibilities for Tanzania was to develop its tourism sector. So, Walter Rodney debated either the vice president or one of the cabinet ministers, someone very high up in the government. The minister argued for tourism and Walter was adamantly against it. The auditorium was packed: standing room only. Everybody came to this debate to see this way of thinking on a problem, and Walter was incisive and incredibly funny.

He pointed out to the minister that when people go to Europe for tourism, they go there to eat French food and French things. But that when they come to Africa, they are not going to eat African food and you would have to import all of that food. So, tourism is not going to be nearly as lucrative or the same kind of endeavor as it is in Europe.

Now, there is a great deal of anthropological work on tourism and what happens to countries in the process of opening up to tourism. In a sense, Walter was very prescient in terms of that work.

He was definitely a gadfly. He could not be controlled. He would say what he thought. He never minced words. He was very truthful according to his likes, to how he saw things. Sometimes he was right and sometimes he was wrong. But I suppose that is not always the most comfortable thing for someone who is such a popular intellectual. He was a popular teacher and with a great following among the students.

When I left Africa in 1972, my first teaching job was at Yale,[3] and I taught "Peoples and Cultures of Africa." Walter's book, *How Europe Underdeveloped Africa*, was an amazing resource. He wrote in the tradition of C. Eric Lincoln[4] and W. E. B. Du Bois.[5] But what was important is that he confronted what was the given wisdom at the time. We call it modernization theory. This is the notion that underdeveloped countries were underdeveloped because of factors intrinsic to themselves—because they did not have democratic political systems or that people didn't work as hard. And that the contact between the colonial world and the West was moving Africa into modernization and was a positive thing.

Walter Rodney's book pointed this out differently. He began the book by saying we are now politely calling these countries developing countries, but, in fact, we should call them underdeveloped countries because they are underdeveloped. He reasoned that they were underdeveloped because someone underdeveloped them. He talked about the relationship between Europe and Africa as of Europe progressively underdeveloping Africa through contact, the slave trade, and so on.

This was a very new view for my students. The fact is he had it so well documented; I know there have been criticisms of the book, but it was well documented and it was a voice in the wilderness in a sense in the way in which people looked at Africa. It was very useful in teaching.

What I find interesting is that his thesis that the Third World has been underdeveloped by its relationship with the West actually predates Immanuel Wallerstein, who in 1974 wrote a book, *The Modern World-System*.[6] His book was read widely in universities and had a tremendous effect on a theoretical approach to colonialism and the West. Walter actually predated him with respect to that thesis, in looking at the relation as a negative one as opposed to a positive one. Both Walter and Wallerstein were going against the view that the relationship was one that benefited Africa. But Walter was the first to point out that the relationship exploited Africa. This really shifted the lens of social scientists in terms of the way in which they began to look at these relationships.

Walter was also, in his work, and certainly in this book, very honest about the negative aspects of African society as well as the positive aspects. What was important about Rodney's work is that he said it was the underlying relationship between African nations, or what became African nations, and the metropole that was responsible for their poverty and underdevelopment: just the fact of the slave trade and taking all those people, which is a major resource, out of Africa. This is still the case. The relationship between Africa and the West is one of exploitation, and until the nature of that relationship changes, things will not change in Africa.

To a great extent, I think Walter is as relevant today as he was at that time. What was important, at the time, was that no one else had put it in that way and said it in such a well-documented way.

8—Issa G. Shivji

I grew up in the eastern region of Tanzania, where I did my primary school. All my secondary school I did in Dar es Salaam—actually, [living] in this very apartment. So I grew up here. Then in 1966 I completed my high school, and in 1967 I joined the university. At that time it was the University College, Dar es Salaam, because it was part of the University of East Africa. 1967 was an important year because the year before there had been a student demonstration that opposed the government's proposal to start National Service, which was mandatory for university students. You had to spend about five months in the camps, and for the next eighteen months 40 percent of your salary would be deducted. Students opposed it. The president, Julius Nyerere, "sent them down": expelled them for a year.

That started a whole rethinking about the university, and there was a big conference on the role of university. Then in February 1967 came the Arusha Declaration.[1] The ruling party, the Tanganyika African National Union [TANU], declared the Arusha Declaration and a policy of socialism and self-reliance. Our word in Kiswahili, *Ujamaa*, became the official policy. A number of companies in the commanding heights of the national economy were nationalized by the government. That started a whole new debate at the university.

Walter Rodney had just come from SOAS[2] and became a young lecturer here. In the conference on rethinking the role of the university in now socialist Tanzania, he played a very important role. So, when I joined the university in July 1967, it was a campus with lots of discussions and debates in which Rodney participated. So that's my background. From 1967 to 1970, I did my Bachelor of Laws degree in the Faculty of Law. I went to England in 1970 to do my master's, came back in 1971, and from '71 to '72 I did my National Service. Since then, I have been at the university and participated in the various debates and writings.

Two years ago [2006], I retired from the Faculty of Law because we have a statutory retirement age of sixty. But I was appointed the Mwalimu Julius Nyerere Chair in Pan-African Studies. It's newly established, and I am the first holder of that chair. So I am back at the university.[3]

I can't recall if Walter came before or after the demonstrations, but he certainly participated in the discussion that followed after the 1966 expulsion and after the Arusha Declaration. After the Declaration, in '67, '68, there was a small group of people called the Socialist Club in which Malawians, Ugandans, Ethiopians, and many other students were involved. The Socialist Club was transformed into the University Students African Revolutionary Front (USARF). It was all the initiative of students, not the faculty. Walter was one of the few young faculty who was involved, but purely within a relationship of equality. There was no professor and student there.

The students were very militant, and the Revolutionary Front, in which I was a member, was led by the chairman, Yuweri Museveni, who is now the president of Uganda, and a number of other comrades were involved in the leadership. Then in 1968 we established the organ of the University Students African Revolutionary Front, which was called *Cheche*. This was a Cyclostyled student journal containing many militant articles and analyses of not only Tanzania but the world situation and the role of young people in the African revolution. In the first issue, Rodney had an article. He wrote something on labor. I too had an article, called "Educated Barbarians." This was our first issue. It actually became, we realized only later, a very important journal circulated as far as the United States. There were some study groups anxiously waiting for the journal to come out. The third issue was a special issue called "The Silent Class Struggle." This was a long essay, written by me, which basically argued that we should not judge socialism simply by listening to what people say, what leaders say, but by what is actually happening in reality: What are the relations of production being created and the class interests involved? So, we worked on the whole question of the development of class and which class is the agency for building socialism. The issue that followed carried commentary on my long essay. One of the comments was by Walter Rodney, and after that the journal was banned and the organization deregistered.

The reasons given were simply that we don't need foreign ideology. We have our own ideology: Ujamaa. *Cheche* is a Kiswahili word. Translated it's "to spark." The *Spark* was Nkrumah's journal, but *Spark* was a translation from *Iskra*, Lenin's journal. So what the students did immediately after that was change the name to *Maji Maji*. Now, *Maji Maji* is a reference to the first revolt, 1905, of the people in Tanganyika and the coast against German imperialism. This was called the Maji Maji War, the Maji Maji Rebellion. The journal continued for some time after that and continued to publish militant articles. Though USARF was banned, many of the leaders of USARF took over the TANU League. The TANU League was the youth arm of the ruling party, and they continued their militant activities.

During ten to fifteen years, beginning in the 1980s, the last period of Mwalimu Nyerere, and particularly the last five years, were very critical. We were engulfed in a serious crisis: economic and political. For the first time, the legitimacy of the political regime was questioned. Since Mwalimu Nyerere stepped down in 1985, the various policies were reversed under pressure from the World Bank, the IMF, and the donors, particularly from Western imperialism. The 1980s were also the beginning of the fall of the Soviet Union.

One of the sights that was attacked, ideologically, was the university. The World Bank was telling Africa you don't need universities, that they were white elephants, and what you needed to do was to place emphasis on primary education. The university was starved of resources. The faculty also began to move out, finding greener pastures either outside the country or in research institutes, consultancies, think tanks, and so on. Much of the period of vigorous debates was heavily affected by the reorientation of the university. The university was turned into a factory to support and answer to the needs of the market. So faculties of commerce and the professional faculties became much more dominant. The last fifteen to twenty years at the university—all the gains of that period have been reversed. One of the objectives of the Nyerere Chair is to try to reclaim to the extent possible the old debates and to reintroduce and redirect the debates on campus.

In the old period, the international context was very different. It was a period high on revolution. You had the civil rights movement in the United States. You had the Vietnam War. The Vietnam War mobilized young people all over the world. You had the French student demonstrations. You had the liberation movements in southern Africa, which were based in Dar es Salaam and strongly supported by Mwalimu Nyerere. The students at the university had very close connections with the liberation movements. Members of USARF went to liberated areas and lived there. All over the world, there were vigorous debates going on. This was the first decade of independence in Africa. The whole meaning of independence for Africans was questioned—is it real independence—and there was talk about neocolonialism.

Some of the texts fondly read were Fanon's[4] *The Wretched of the Earth*, Nkrumah's[5] *Neo-Colonialism, The Last Stage of Imperialism*, texts by Samir Amin,[6] Paul Baran,[7] and Paul Sweezy.[8] These were the kinds of things read, and also classics of Marxism. So the international context was certainly at a high point all over the world. One interesting example of the kind of contradictory situation we had, we had a seminar of East and Central Africa youth organized under the youth league of the party. It was held at Nkrumah Hall at the university. A lot of our comrades delivered papers. Rodney also delivered a paper. At that time, there were the hijackings by the Palestine Liberation Organization. His paper referred to that. It was a very militant paper about the African revolution and so on and castigating the first independent regimes as petit bourgeois regimes that had hijacked the revolution. He called it the "briefcase revolution," where the leaders went to Lancaster House,[9] compromised, and came back with independence and this was not real independence.

This paper was published in the party [TANU] paper called *The Nationalist.* Nyerere took a very strong objection. The next day the paper carried an editorial called, "Revolutionary Hot Air,"[10] and in very strong terms attacked Rodney for preaching violence to young people. It basically said that while, of course, we were trying to build a socialist society, our socialist society would be built on our own concrete conditions, and you cannot simply become the apse and cannot preach violence and violent overthrow of brotherly African governments. He said Rodney is welcome to stay here but not to preach violence to young people. When that editorial appeared, I remember the morning the papers came out, we read the editorial and all of us suspected, until more was confirmed, that that editorial was written by President Nyerere himself. So we had prepared this special issue of *Maji Maji* in which all the papers would be carried. One of our comrades, when he read the editorial, became so scared that he took all the papers we collected and burned them, and in the process scorched the front grass lawn near student dormitories.

Then Rodney replied in a long letter, a very interesting letter. Basically, he defended himself, but he was also appeasing in that he was thankful and grateful he was allowed to stay here and that when he talked about capitalism and neocolonialism he was only talking about that system which carried his ancestors as slaves into other parts of the world, and now he was trying to establish a reconnection and talk about this gruesome system which is still with us.

His famous book, *How Europe Underdeveloped Africa,* was written here. If you look at the preface of that book, there are two people he thanks personally for reading the manuscript and both of them happen to be students, Karim Hirji and Henry Mapolu. That was the relationship we had with Walter. Museveni knew him very well. Museveni was also a student of political science.

After 1967, one of the important movements started by the students themselves was that knowledge cannot be compartmentalized. It's holistic, and whether you are doing science or law or political science, the knowledge must be integrated. The Faculty of Law was the first to start a course called "Problems of East Africa," in which lecturers from different departments participated, and Rodney was one of them. That course then evolved into what was known as a "common course," which was compulsory for all the students coming into the university. That further evolved into what became the Institute of Development Studies and later it became the Institute of East African Social and Economic Problems. These were common courses in the formal syllabi. But we the students had our own ideological classes. We met every Sunday, and we were assigned readings; some came with readings, made presentations, everyone participated to do what we call "arm ourselves" ideologically. Again, Rodney was a prominent participant in these ideological classes. This was totally voluntary. What we read and discussed was then taken to the classroom. We would not allow lecturers to get away with anything without being challenged.

So debates continued outside the classroom and inside the classroom, and there was a close relationship with the liberation movements. All the important leaders of the liberation movements came to the university, gave lectures, participated in debates, from Eduardo Mondlane[11] to Gora Ibrahim[12] of the Pan-African Congress [PAC]. I remember Stokely Carmichael came. C. L. R. James came to Dar es Salaam and gave fantastic lectures for a whole week. Cheddi Jagan[13] from Guyana came and gave a lecture. East African leaders, including Oginga Odinga,[14] came and gave a lecture. The "Front" never missed an opportunity. Whatever events took place in Africa, there would be a statement by the "Front" analyzing and taking a position on it. The USARF positions were taken very seriously by the liberation movements. Samora Machel came and talked to the students. There would not be a single night without some lecture taking place.

There was a time when there was a bit of a split. This was much more internal, and particularly because in that period the split was a reaction to the split in international socialism, between China and the Soviet Union. The Dar es Salaam campus followed very closely that debate of either the Communist Party of China or the Communist Party of the Soviet Union: the rising socialist imperialism. We had lots of discussions on that. But many of them were internal within our groups.

This idea that Rodney left Dar es Salaam because of, or just ahead of, an order to leave—I do not think it's true. If it was true, he would have definitely told us. Don't forget, Rodney left early and went to Jamaica. From Jamaica he was deported. That's where he wrote his very famous pamphlet, *Groundings with My Brothers*. After the riots in Jamaica, he came back to Dar es Salaam. Then he left in 1974. Now, when he was about to leave, I remember specifically a personal conversation. We were driving from the campus, and at the time he and Pat were preparing to leave for Guyana. I told Walter, I said, "Walter, why do you have to go? Look, stay here. You can easily try and get your citizenship and continue the struggle. You don't have to go back." He said, "No, comrade. I can make my contribution here, but I will not be able ever to grasp the idiom of the people. I will not be able to connect easily. I have to go back to the people I know and who know me." I heeded that. That was his position and he left.

Then during the Zimbabwe independence celebration—he had returned to Guyana and formed the Working People's Alliance and we closely followed it—on his way to Zimbabwe, and this was a time when the movement was in trouble, he passed through and stayed with one of our comrades here. This comrade told him, "Walter, stay, don't go back. Guyana is dangerous." There was a case against him in court. Walter said, "No, I cannot just run away. I have to go back." So it is certainly not true that he was pushed out.

It's more believable that he was pulled because he felt he could make his contribution there, in Guyana. And he did, in my view. One can make critical assessments in hindsight, but one of the things we appreciated, and came to learn from, the party, the Working People's Alliance managed to bring together Indian and African youth. This was a real breakthrough. Of course, there were other problems. So my own view is that [Walter being forced out of Tanzania] could not be true. If so, we would have known.

Even at that time, while we understood Rodney's background, the comrades here sometimes did not fully subscribe to his positions on race. We often told him that while it was understood in the North American situation, here it could not be applied. Another issue where we had strong disagreement was a piece he wrote called "Ujamaa as Scientific Socialism." This was the early seventies. He was trying to show, drawing on the Narodniks,[15] that Ujamaa is scientific socialism. Before he published that, we met and had a discussion on his draft. We had some heated exchanges and vigorously disagreed with him. We argued that you cannot identify petit bourgeois socialism as scientific socialism. At the end of it, Rodney said he would defer to his Tanzanian comrades since we were the ones who knew the situation here. He went ahead and published it. We did not expect he would. So what I am trying to say, coming from a different background, is that we did not accept everything with unanimity.

But we realized Walter was an institution. Whenever we had differences we met internally and sorted it out. He left a huge shadow here, on the left, on the African left, and in Tanzania itself. His own learning and foundation were laid here. When he came to Dar es Salaam, he came essentially as a young academic from SOAS, where he had just finished his Ph.D. His years here were an important period of formation of his own ideas. Like it was an important period for the rest of us. I think his international fame came after the book and, of course, was connected with what happened in Jamaica.

Walter Rodney after Dar es Salaam

I'll try to be as fair as possible. My own view is there were aspects of Rodney's organization inclination which I think, in a sense, exposed him. Of course, a powerful movement like that is bound to have enemies. But I am not quite sure if Rodney always paid enough attention: to a matter of tactics, number one, and number two, to security of the leadership. It does happen with powerful leaders like Rodney, the movement tends to become very dependent on single leaders. That is one lesson to draw. When that leader goes, invariably the movement falls apart. That's what seems to have happened in Guyana. While in theory, of course, we talk about the importance of the movement, importance of the people, importance of the working people, in practice we always find it difficult to build movements which can continue regardless of original leadership.

Of course, I do not know at the moment, and I keep asking people from there, if there has been a critical assessment of the WPA. I haven't seen one myself. I also get the feeling that once Rodney went and the movement fell apart, even the leaders seemed to disintegrate. I am not sure if any of them have gone back and tried to reassess it.

While Walter was militant in the Guyana situation, if anything, the impression I got—and I consider this to be his contribution—was being able to build a mass movement. I may be wrong. But I always took the WPA to be a mass movement and not an underground conspiratorial group. If at a certain point the WPA, after assessment, reached the conclusion that there was no other way except armed struggle, I don't know. I never really came across an assessment. But certainly, from what we know and the way it operated, the image I have of the WPA is Rodney as its collective leader. Another very interesting contribution of the WPA: collective leadership, with all the mass of youth behind them, walking the streets, going to a sugar plantation. This is the image I have of the WPA. That image is not totally consistent with some kind of conspiratorial group and armed struggle.

But there are two aspects, particularly for the period we are going through now: collective leadership and a mass movement are important contributions, something to learn from. Not to ignore the circumstances connected with armed struggle, but I think one thing we have learned is that armed struggle alone, without a mass movement, has a tendency to deteriorate. And once again the importance of politics rather than militarism is coming back. I remember in the early eighties I was on a lecture tour in the United States and Canada, and the point I kept emphasizing was that the period we were going through in Africa then was essentially a period of the insurrection of ideas, insurrection of mass movements, open mass movements, rather than underground armed struggle groups: in other words, insurrectional politics. To a certain extent we saw insurrectional politics in the movement that started after the fall of the Berlin Wall and the so-called democratization movement. In West Africa and elsewhere, it became a mass movement.

Of course, it was suppressed, preempted; it was hijacked in many ways. What was essentially insurrectional politics for real democracy was hijacked into multiparties. Multiparties is not the end-all of democracy. The liberal Western model cannot simply be adopted, in my view. But those ten to fifteen years of liberal politics and neoliberal economics, I think, are coming to an end. The neoliberal honeymoon is over. Interestingly, there is a whole new, other way of thinking.

Let me give you my own experience in this country. In the few events I organized under the Nyerere Chair, it's amazing to see how young people want to know more about where we are coming from. For that purpose, today, we are beginning to see people talking about the historical experience, talking about Ujamaa.[16] At one time, Ujamaa had become a term of abuse. Nyerere used to say, "If I was to talk about Ujamaa openly I would be considered a fool. I can only whisper about it." But now these ideas are coming back. They are being recalled. In my view, the whole imperialist, neoliberal onslaught is coming to an end. Of course, it won't happen tomorrow. But it doesn't hold the same ideological pull it once supposedly held.

There is a lot of rethinking going on in the world. All over Latin America we are witnessing it. So it's an interesting period.

Now, I don't think we can repeat or just reclaim the past, of course, but we will learn from it and people will want to know where we are coming from.

The current situation in Africa also points to some of the problems of old and the old debates we had. While individuals play an important role, individuals do not necessarily characterize the whole movement. Individuals do get transformed once they get into power. A very good example is our own Yuweri Museveni, who was a militant, a Fanonist actually, during the student days and what he has become. I think to understand it much more we must view it in terms of the social, political, economic forces of the time. In the case of Mugabe, we have to go back to history. ZANU's[17] accession to power was a kind of compromise. In which some of the African leaders I know of were involved, including Nyerere. They pushed ZANU to accept that compromise. You will notice—and more work has to be done on this—that in the case of liberation movements, at very critical times, in South Africa, in Zimbabwe, some of the important leaders who held a clear vision of what they wanted their societies to be, these leaders were bumped off: Hani,[18] in the ANC, in Zimbabwe, Herbert Chitepo.[19]

When these leaders came to power, they inherited the state structures. Look, for example, at Zimbabwe. The "Lancaster compromise" meant that for ten years they could not touch the land occupied by white settlers. Land was the leading issue for which the people fought. And Mugabe did not take action. The new people that came to power began to develop themselves into a class of their own, so to speak. The land question had to be addressed. But by the time he addressed it, and the way he addressed it, that led to the situation we are in. To the extent that now you cannot even mobilize your own people to support your anti-imperialist stand. So anything said is just rhetoric. There are complex issues of how those leaders addressed those issues. Particularly in Africa, we notice that when progressive leaders come to power, they find themselves in difficulty because they have not been rooted in the people and do not take the messages of the people. Without knowing the pulse of the people, they immediately become alienated. They become prisoners of the structures they inherited.

So there is a lot to be said about movements that may look protected, confused, but are movements from below. It remains to be seen to what extent the left, or revolutionary elite, will learn from that movement, integrate themselves in it, before they claim to know and to teach. There is a lot of learning, a lot of learning, to be done.

9—Clive Yolande Thomas

Walter and I—it was more than serendipity. In fact, I went to Tanzania because Walter urged me to go. At that point they were looking for a professor of economics, and he was among a few scholars who felt that they should get someone from the Third World. It was a suggestion initiated by Walter and some of his comrades that I would be the ideal person to to be visiting professor for the academic year. When I went there, that was the period I became very familiar with Walter. We actually became friends.

Prior to that, our paths crossed. For example, when I was in Jamaica, I was a lecturer at the UWI when he was banned from returning to Jamaica. I took part in the protest of that banning, and I was then fired from the university and refused entry into Jamaica, and that is how I came to be in Guyana. So my coming to Guyana was a direct result of his being banned, after a conference in Montreal,[1] from returning to Jamaica. After coming to Guyana, I remained there and through his initiative I went to Tanzania.

But when I was in Tanzania, I managed to convince Walter of one thing. I told him that there is a limit to which, if you are not a national of the territory, not born there, or not a full citizen, you can really participate in the social, economic, and political life of the country. I urged him to come back to Guyana. He gave me a sort of understanding that he would consider that, and therefore I took the initiative when I returned to Guyana. I was also chairman of the University of Guyana Workers' Union, and I took the initiative to move for him to be visiting professor at the University of Guyana. The position was approved by the appointments commission of the university to come to Guyana, and they issued a letter of appointment.

When he came to Guyana, again almost by way of coincidence, he was refused a job. So we started out with a series of protests to try to get him appointed to the university, which culminated in a lot of political events in Guyana: the formation of the WPA, and eventually his assassination. So our paths crossed at very important points in our lives. I think it had a lot to do with the fact we were both academics who were activists. But I was not, initially, as activist-oriented as he was. My activism developed as a result of having to do some struggling over his situation. And also because, being in touch with him, I became convinced that one had to blend theory with practice. I felt the commitments. I had to follow through. In keeping with the ideas I believed in, it was required that I constantly engage myself with broader social, political, and other issues, cultural issues in the society, and I would like to believe I am able to maintain that.

That's how I met Ralph Gonsalves.[2] He was a student leader; very few lecturers participated in the student protest around Rodney's banning in Jamaica. The protest was led by the student leaders. I probably distinguished myself in his eyes, and certainly became known to him because I was a lecturer who was willing to participate in street protest. That was a very important engagement between the two of us, and since then we have always remained in some contact even though he became prime minister. Because it stemmed from those early days of fighting together to have Walter reestablished as a professor at the UWI. I understand Trinidad's prime minister, Patrick Manning, was also part of the protest, but I don't recall him. I don't recall him at all. But that is probably more a comment on my limited experiences with the students than his activism. But I don't recall him being very up front in these activities.

Walter came at an important point in time in the development of a Caribbean sense of sovereignty, commitment, and vocation. I think, then, many people who were just going into the period of independence wanted to find a different path toward development and to make a contribution to civilization in a different way. We felt the world was really our oyster. We really were doing things that were different from what had happened previously, historically, and that our generation would make a difference. So many of the people of our generation were motivated to do something toward the development of a more prosperous society, and certainly to reestablish dignity and development of the West Indian people. That was primary. So that was a very important generation and everybody who passed through that period, I think, was in one way or the other affected by currents.

I personally feel that the battles we won in that period were to a large extent subsequently lost. The global world system is a powerful one, and global capitalism has become inexorable. It has now developed to globalization, and it's a very international and very powerful means of domination of all countries, and particularly ones that are small, as in the Caribbean. Even the mighty states like the United States and China have to respond to it, but not to the extent we do. So it's very difficult in this context to assert a true ascendancy of the national will or the national preference or the people's identity or the people's culture and so forth. It is very, very difficult. So we've always as a result tended to frame our struggles for West Indian independence, West Indian integration, as an effort to put us into a unit so we can engage the world, so that the world wouldn't make us perish.

But at that time we had a more positive orientation. It was not only defensive, trying to defend ourselves in the global environment, but we had a more assertive, positive, proactive view that we could make a contribution to civilization. That was a part of Walter that was very important. It was the part of his vision that kept me going during that period. I think it was shared by many persons, and is one I maintain up to this point in time. It's the truly important one.

And that is why I feel very disappointed when people argue in favor of West Indian integration, West Indian political unity, as if it were to prevent us from perishing. I don't think, at the economic level, that we would perish if we did not integrate. Because if we look at countries like the British Virgin Islands and the American Virgin Islands, these are all colonial territories and the people there consider themselves to be prosperous. And any one of them has poverty lines drawn at $30,000 per year, when many countries like Haiti cannot even attain one dollar a day. In Guyana the poverty line is drawn at just about $1.50 a day. So there is a vast difference, and people can achieve a level of economic prosperity in these states. What I think they suffer from is a certain cultural impoverishment, and that was what we were recognizing.

So we argued then that the case for integration, although it had economic dimensions, was really a cultural case: a case based on our contributions to humanity. I don't think that we can easily forget that this, the Caribbean, was the cradle of capitalism. We really forged in many ways through the plantation, and through slavery, through all those experiences, the prototypical capitalistic institutions. At the period of time these things were taking place, they were at the cutting edge, as it were, of social advance, much like the transnationals would have been twenty to thirty years ago. I think we were trying to recover that kind of importance not driven by outside domination but by internal attempts to promote the capacity of the people who lived through these experiences.

The Caribbean Single Market [CSM] and the Caribbean Single Market Economy [CSME] are to my mind one continuum, going all the way up to political unity. I really do feel that the region needs to be a single political unit. But that requires such a gigantic leap in terms of political vision and political willingness to sacrifice considerations like sovereignty, as currently interpreted, that I think it is beyond the ilk of this current generation of Caribbean leadership. We were thinking that we might be the generation of political leaders that would have made that possible. But, of course, we failed miserably, and the failing was not really because of the fault of other people, but the fault of ourselves. We lacked the capacity. We didn't learn enough. We didn't have enough patience. We did not have a lot of other things that would have been required to sustain our struggle to make this a different place.

Yet our achievements are hard to deny. It is really something singular and particular to the ideas we represented and the hope we sought to express. I would prefer to see it in those terms: part of the grandiose effort to do something different to make a difference to our community. Maybe we were aspiring to too much. I don't know. I do not often articulate my own feelings in this way. Maybe it's the camera that has made me express a more personal view of some of these things that I would otherwise have done in a pure exchange in terms of a lecture or a formal presentation.

I am sure I could not have convinced Walter, on my own, to return home. But I think when I mentioned it to him, it was at the right time. He himself was coming around to it. He was pretty active in Tanzania. He was active at the level of ideological exchanges and writing in the press and teaching the young people about ideology. He ran political classes. In fact, he asked me to come and contribute to the classes, and that became the subject of my book, *Dependence and Transformation*,[3] which was very important at that time. It was dedicated to the people of Tanzania and to the students of that class. From time to time, Walter had friction with the government. That is what made me feel there was a limit he could go to as a non-citizen. Because when frictions came up, ultimately there is a point when it will be asked, should a non-national be entitled to make that level of political interference?

At home, the central trust was to raise the people: people's power. Even though it may be cast in black power, the central component was still people's power. Walter would not limit it to black people's power in a multiracial society. He recognized that in some societies he may not be able to speak of multiracial power without first asserting that the power of a significant minority would be actively repressed by the state, and I think that was the American context. But when he came to Guyana, it was never difficult because Guyana was always seen as black: as being nonwhite. But not even being nonwhite, but really being people's power because there was no strong white oligarchic element resident in Guyana.

On a personal level, what I learned from him throughout the years were games. Because in Tanzania they had very limited opportunities for the typical entertainment you get in the Caribbean, all the clubs and that type of thing, and he spent a lot of time playing games. He loved his games at home and playing them with his family, and we played a lot of them together. He wasn't a big beach person because when one went on safaris or tours like that, one was more often with the expatriates from Europe who saw Africa in those terms and wanted to do a lot of exploring. I never went with him on a safari or anything like that, but I did go on trips and excursions with the people from England, America, other parts of Europe, and so on, who were resident in Tanzania and picking up on the African experience.

I happened to be in Trinidad the night he died. I had gone over there, I can't remember what it was about—it was about the party or something to do with the party, and then I got the phone call. It was like a daze, and then I had to come back. I can remember the funeral ceremony and certainly the funeral service. I mean, I nearly broke down; it was quite a moving experience, because it was an ecumenical service and it was a Catholic cathedral.

During that period where we were fearful for our lives, a very good friend of mine was a Roman Catholic priest, a Jesuit superior, in the Caribbean and in Guyana, Father Malcolm Rodrigues, who used to put me up every night. He was responsible for my safety. And I slept more nights than I would like to remember somewhere in the Jesuit sanctuary, in some room or bed, whatever arrangement he could make for me. So, that's how we survived during that period, because of the fear that attempts would be made to assassinate us. In fact, one was made directly at me, an attempt to kidnap me from my house.

I was living on a street, one away from here, and a police car came up early in the morning, at about four o'clock, and they said I was wanted at the police station and to come down. But the police station didn't send the car, because after I came out and he told me that, I went back in the house and sneakily phoned the police and asked if they were looking for Clive Thomas. And they said they didn't know what I am talking about. So, I just had to stall them and pretend as if I was getting dressed to come and never emerged from the house. Also at that time, in fact it was a few years after, Joshua Ramsammy[4] was outside the bank and they came and shot him, right outside the bank. So at that time the Burnham regime was quite determined to assassinate us as a means of silencing the opposition to the regime.

There were several other WPA people who were killed. Ohene Koama, who was a very important activist, the police stopped him just around the corner by the gardens. They asked him to open his trunk, and then they shot him point-blank and just left him. There were quite a few executions, and many people were fearful for their life. I mean, Ramsammy survived with a bullet that went into his lungs. We had to visit him in the hospital, and all that, and guard him there. Then, after that, we had a lot of guards. People would volunteer to guard us, but we were never comfortable with those arrangements because the guards, you never know where they come from. So, I felt that the only real cover we had was political cover.

That's when I decided I would continue writing and become even bolder and bolder in my public pronouncements. So that the political price of assassinating me would be higher. I don't know if that acted as a deterrent or they didn't think I was important enough, but it certainly prevented further attack. I have continued that way even now, when it has almost gotten dangerous to voice strong views on the current regime. That is another thing Walter would have been disappointed in; with the fall of the PNC dictatorship we really have not been able to transcend the limitations of Guyana racial politics. The traditional divisions we've had and are still contending with now involve us in a certain state degeneration that in many ways is worse and even more brutal than what existed in the PNC regime.

I mean, it has become more brutal largely because of the techniques for the management of our population by the state, and the arms of the security services, and surveillance capability, and all that, which have grown by multiple degrees. This regime is willing to sanction, or support, allow to prosper, shadowy groups that are involved in extrajudicial killings linked to the narcotics trade, and that has become a very deadly combination. In fact, I wrote about this. I started a series of articles called "The Rise of the Criminal State,"[5] where I've been arguing that what is happening in Guyana is the state is being transformed into a vehicle for criminal enterprise, which draws in the antecedent PNC authoritarian state, of course. Part of it is contradictory, but it also takes into account the new situation. The global environment, transnationalized crime, the narco-economy—these things can thrive and have more mobility, more capacity to prosper. And the ruling regime finds it convenient or expedient to form alliances to prevent it from being overthrown by what they think is politically inspired violence.

If they felt all along that the violence coming from the streets or in the streets has a political basis because it's largely by Africans, it must be connected to the PNC. So they'd be willing to go into alliances with drug cartels to maintain rule, and this has been a deadly combination. Because I think it's very, very bad when the narco elements invade police and invade the army and all that, which is happening in Latin America. But I think it becomes most dangerous when it involves the political establishment, because it's very hard to root it out because of their ineffective control. But what is happening now, the situation is changing a bit because the Americans are definitely seeking to rendition more and more of them, as is happening with a few cases going before U.S. courts. So we don't know what is going to happen. But that's another story, far removed from Walter.

Walter would probably turn in his grave to see us in such a situation where we'd be discussing this today. Because certainly when we talked and thought about Guyana in that period of time, nobody could have envisioned such a pathological degeneration—nobody. It was inconceivable. I mean, I could not believe that people were doing this, who sometimes were my students, and be transformed in this way. So, I would say one of the lessons I've learned from that experience, although secondhand, is that corrosive power and the corruptive power of the state is enormous. And once they were there, to maintain power at any means, after a while the means justify the ends and the ends justify the means, and so you become more and more degenerate in your responses. But the Burnham regime was pretty brutal, and we thought, you know, that it was the epitome of darkness. But now, in retrospect, few of us would still maintain that position, given the current situation, because we've certainly had experiences where it's become, in that sense, worse.

But I wouldn't go so far as to say that we have a worse economic, social, and political situation than we had then, because certainly the economy has picked up, if not grown. People are not suffering from the physical outages and the shortages and the rampant inflation that characterized the period in the 1980s with Burnham and the repression we had. Yeah, it might be drug money, but I think there's a difference between the levels of security that individuals feel in terms of economic support now. I mean, we could not sit down here in those days and have this filming going on without a power outage or without serious problems happening. The phone would not have rung as often as it has because it would probably not be working. It's very popular among analysts of the Caribbean to argue that the crisis we face now is the worst we've had since independence. But I think the crisis in the '80s was worse, because it had a level of physical deprivation that current crises do not present to the poor masses of the population. Yes, they still have a sense that as a last resort they could go to a shop and steal a pound of flour. But in those days, you could go to the shop and it would not have anything in it. I mean, I certainly knew I was taking risks and I certainly felt fearful and I tried to make the risks as calculated as possible. But I really don't think anybody collectively voiced the view that death was imminent.

I never had any contact with him, Gregory Smith,[6] and that's surprising. I never met him. The first time I heard of him was after Walter's assassination. But Moses Bhagwan[7] called me last night, and he mentioned something I didn't know about, which if you get a chance to interview him up in New York you might be able to pursue. He said that Gregory Smith made attempts to get into the party through him. Moses was in charge of mass activities like organizing public meetings and public events and so on. And he said on different occasions Gregory Smith was increasingly impatient about being able to contribute to the party and become active within the mass group, and Smith had mentioned in particular that he had electronic skills the party could find useful. But Moses told me what he had done secretly without the guy's knowledge, because instinctively he felt Smith was pushing too hard. He asked his nephew, who was working at Telecoms[8] then, to check out whether Gregory Smith was an employee because he posed as an employee of Telecoms. But they couldn't find a trace of anybody who knows him or knows the person. So Moses was in a sense also playing a game with Smith, putting him off, putting him off. He kept coming back. But what Bhagwan didn't know, of course, was that this man Smith was seeing Walter. I told Moses maybe he went to Walter and told him that he tried to get in through you and that we were negligent or something like that.

Gregory Smith wrote a book. I really don't know if I should give it credence, you know, by just reading it or even considering it.[9] But from the excerpts I've seen some of the things he said are so preposterous that they defy common sense. And the dates are so confusing. I mean, he said he was hiding out in Brickdam.[10] And I find that incredible because that place was hiding me out. Haha. Of all the places to pick, and. moreover, what was worse is that the Jesuits, more than anybody, actively believed he was a killer. And they, through the *Catholic Standard*, were more active than anybody in Guyana, including us, in pursuing him as a murderer. One thing I can tell you about them is that once they committed to a cause or an issue, they're relentless. I mean, they don't give in easily. They see it almost as God's will for them to pursue these things. What Malcolm [Rodrigues] did—he used to put me up every single night and hide me out. So how could Smith be hiding—and nobody could do anything at that level of security—without Malcolm being involved?

Because he would be the contact person in the trenches all the time. He would move people, move us, and do all sorts of things during that period. It was a real committed thing to the Guyana cause.

So, of course, we don't have anything against the Smith family. As we, the WPA, made clear in our review of the book, I mean, we don't heap the sins of the brother onto the other sister. We would never do that. I mean, that's not part of the WPA's culture. So we're willing to forgive them, treat them fairly and respectfully. But if his sister wants to associate us with the libelous things they are saying, well that's a different thing. We'll have to criticize it intellectually. We don't make her a victim; we don't blame her for the murder. Whatever he told her that persuaded her to take that point of view I don't know, but it has to be someone who is very unfamiliar with details. You can't be walking around in Georgetown during that period casually like that. It was a very, very tense period. They even had me wait in Trinidad for a couple of days [after Walter's death] before I came in. And from the time I landed, security was following me, very overt.

Smith's book suggests there was a WPA conspiracy to kill Walter, and that the WPA spirited Smith out of the country. And it's something that we had all that influence and control, the police and the army, amazing. I mean, the most influence we had was maybe at the level of a couple of captains, a few sergeants—and nobody from the upper hierarchy of the military. A few police officers, maybe at the rank-and-file level, maybe a couple of them educated, but none we could look back in retrospect and say were WPA moles or covert WPA people inside the military security apparatus, or it would have surfaced by now. They could not have survived there for so long, or they would have been prominent people or something like that. So, Smith was assuming we had power to write and make passports and all that. I suspect Burnham might have truly believed we had that capacity, when it was not the case, which may have accounted for his preemptive act, given Walter's trip to Africa shortly before his death.

Yeah, but crossing over to Suriname by ferry, anybody could pull that scam. I know people who go over there and shop every weekend, and you know they're not supposed to be traveling through that route. They go on a Saturday and come back on a Monday or Tuesday. It's very very easy to cross "backtrack"[11] without being inspected. All you have to do is take a regular taxi going up to Springlands and the touts will meet you and ask if you want a boat and before you can blink an eye you could be on a boat and gone.

You see, I always felt we never had any real support from many of those outside governments that look to be progressive. They always felt that we were being too harsh on Burnham. Burnham was not as bad as others; they'd say things like that. Even Bishop[12] in Grenada, who would have been closest to us in the days he was planning to achieve the transfer of power in Grenada, he never sanctioned any support for the WPA once he was in power. He made a few statements, but we wanted finance, we wanted equipment, and we were still publishing with a Cyclostat. We never got a printery or a printing press. We were really, if you look at the mechanics of the party, a party that was 90 percent financed by the contributions of the activist group. You're talking about tens of dollars and twenties. You're not talking about any million-dollar effort.

But I always used to think at the beginning—something Andaiye[13] reminded me of—that these guys don't see Burnham as less than progressive. Compared to those they saw around the world, Burnham was no devil. They saw him as being persuasive and willing to do things to champion the leftist cause, the progressive cause. And Burnham was very clever that way, to insert himself into these things. He's also good with people in the traditional areas of power. There was somebody in the Commonwealth, among the prime minister group, who had a very detailed conversation with me and told me that Margaret Thatcher liked Burnham as a person. Because he would do things others wouldn't do. He'd go up and almost like flirt with her, make nice facetious comments about how attractive she looked. Burnham knew how to play the game, so he was never isolated by the international community because of what was happening at home. The Cubans certainly never isolated him, and they were a big part of the scene because Russians were not very active in Guyana matters. Fidel, even though he was closely affiliated to the PPP because he belonged to the Communist group, still did not break ranks in any significant way with Burnham.

Regionally, leaders remained cordial and even involved me. Manley[14] was faced with a dilemma about what to do when the economic crisis began unfolding regarding his Central Bank and he asked Burnham, of all people, if he could facilitate getting me to Jamaica so he could have discussions and benefit from my advice. He wanted us all to meet and discuss it together. And Burnham actually called me and put me on a plane, a GDF[15] plane, to take me to Jamaica. It was one of those propeller planes that took maybe a day to get there. A couple of things surprised me about that meeting. One was that the governor, Arthur Brown, who was also the financial secretary of the Central Bank, had a daily program showing how the foreign exchange of Jamaica would be depleted in another fourteen or fifteen days. And you know, he had given that information to the IMF and the World Bank before he even discussed it with the prime minister. I commented that that was amazing for a government that was dealing with the IMF people. Because they had information from the inside as to how much time they had to play with. Brown thought it was the natural thing to do. That was the level of thinking and lack of perceptiveness that came from those establishment technocrats at the time.

The technocrats always felt the outside world were friends of the country, not their opponents in crucial matters. Manley did not want to go into an IMF program. But he had to try to show the inevitability. Once the IMF and the World Bank saw that feature, they knew that the longer they waited the more certain it would happen. Of course, Manley eventually had to turn to the IMF.

10—Rupert Roopnaraine

The trip to Zimbabwe[1] in Walter's life, and certainly as we think back over the weeks and months before the assassination, seems to grow in significance. Getting Walter to Zimbabwe was, of course, a horrendous task. We were at the time leading members of the WPA, all under twenty-four-hour surveillance. We were routinely changing cars, sleeping in different beds every night, and so on. We had to get him from here to Zimbabwe. The decision was taken, and it was kept to a very tight group that knew about it. Obviously, Pat[2] and Bro, Eusi,[3] myself, and that was it. We operated on a very strict need-to-know basis, because it was such a tense and difficult mission. We had, first of all, to get him from Georgetown to the Courantyne [River]. That in itself was really a monstrous task. So we had to go overland. We used about three cars to get him as far as Rosignol. At Rosignol, instead of taking the ferry that we knew would be under surveillance, we used a small fishing boat, and got across to New Amsterdam. From there we had to then go all the way up to the Courantyne, switching cars several times again until we got him to Crabwood Creek. From Crabwood Creek, we took a small fishing boat, in the dead of night, to Nickerie.

At the time, the Sergeants' revolt in Suriname had happened. Bouterse[4] and a number of leaders of the Surinamese Revolution were very close to us, in the sense that they seemed to be a genuine anti-imperialist movement. They had a very strong multiracial outlook. They were against the old politics that had brought Suriname to so much disaster. There were obvious affinities between the WPA and the Sergeants' revolt. We'd had a previous contact after the revolt; they had sent an emissary to Georgetown who had actually spoken with me and with Walter. I won't bother to name them at this stage. So we'd had previous contact with them. But when Walter got to Nickerie, it was up to the Surinamese authorities to move him. They were able to facilitate that. They gave him an entry stamp, and from everything we know from the Zimbabwean episode, Burnham was in a state of shock to find Walter there. One, he had assumed Walter was safely locked down in Guyana. As you know, we had been charged with arson. We were all out on bail. We could not leave the jurisdiction. And there was Walter. Not only was he in Zimbabwe in the flesh, he was really being treated as an African prince. This did not go down very well.

Burnham by that time had earned his spurs and established his credentials as a supporter of the African liberation movement. We [Guyana] were very active in the nonaligned movement. We were chairing the council for Namibia. We had really paid our dues, and he had a right to expect to be treated with some particular attention. Well, Walter was of course very close to the African revolutionaries, a great deal of resentment was built up at that time by Burnham. In fact, I know many people who believe the decision to kill Walter occurred to Burnham when Walter was in Zimbabwe, when he felt this had gone too far. He would not deal with this anymore. I am not so sure myself. It may have been a factor influencing it, no doubt. There were more profound things, I think, influencing the decision. Anyway, Walter then came back from Zimbabwe.

It was a very difficult decision for us in the WPA, very divisive. There were people who walked out of the executive on this issue because they felt, once again, we had been too leaderless[5] on everything.We had undertaken this massive security operation, we had not informed anybody in the leadership, and it caused a lot of consternation in the party. We felt that we had to do it the way we did it. We did not report to the party's executive until Walter was safely back in Guyana.

At the time he came back, I was living in New Garden Street. I remember him coming to see me, and it occurred to me that I had never seen Walter more depressed. There may have been some reasons. He had gone to Zimbabwe with the hopes of getting some kind of assistance from Mugabe and from some of the African comrades. That did not happen, mostly for good logistical reasons, but the fact is he had been very disappointed with the trip as far as assistance to the Guyana revolution. Whether or not that fed into it, I think he was beginning to feel the civil rebellion had ebbed; the high points we had reached after August, September, November, those heroic months of the revolt, things had been beaten back. The revolution was at very low ebb at that stage. I think he felt more impelled to get it going again.

He was a person who really got nourished by the mass movement. I remember Walter saying to me that there was nothing that gave him more nourishment than the trips taken to teach the bauxite workers political economy. He always came back very energized with this contact with ordinary working people who were progressive and on a revolutionary path. This is what really energized him as an activist. I think he felt—there had been the arrest of the brothers on the West Coast, charged for treason—the repression was in full force. He felt that if we did not do something about reigniting the mass movement, it would be lost. At that stage he had hoped that whatever assistance he was hoping to get from Africa would have tipped the balance in favor of the insurrection. When that didn't happen, he was in a very low place, morale had dropped. It was not the first time.Walter was always very sensitive about the need for a certain level of militancy. I chose the occasion of the James lecture to take issue with some of the conclusions that C. L. R. had reached in his very famous essay, "Rodney and the Question of Power." I remember being very disturbed by that thing, when I first read it, because this was not something written by just anyone. This was something written by C. L. R., for whom Walter was one of his disciples, one of his students. I came to the conclusion that the essay was written out of a great deal of pain and affection. It really was something written out of love and a sense of deep, deep, human loss.

But I felt that C. L. R. had come to some conclusions in that essay that were not up to his usual high, high standards of proof and demonstration. For instance, he says in there that we did not know anything about the taking of power and why we didn't—the Suriname coup had just happened—send somebody to Suriname. He said, "You can walk to Suriname." In fact, we were very close to Suriname, as I just indicated—a lot of areas in his essay are like that. It's not that we didn't study those things. But there were concrete conditions here that we were trying to deal with. Guyana did not have any kind of clandestine military arrangements. This is not Latin America. You would give an activist a gun, and the next thing you know, he is threatening his wife with it. They would get into the rum shops, and there was a lot of loose talk. We didn't have any of those traditions, and it made life difficult.

We were at the time attempting to equip ourselves, essentially ready ourselves, and ready the masses for an insurrectionary attack on the state. I make no excuses about that, and I think that the time is fast approaching where more of that would have to become public. I know that in a review in the *Stabroek News* of Gregory Smith's sister's book[6] one of the things they were saying was that there is a need for the commission of enquiry and for it to have the WPA explain more of what it is about. We have said time and time again we are very happy to explain what it is we are about. But the WPA cannot set up a one-party truth and reconciliation committee. Everybody has to come, and, provided everybody comes, we will tell our part of it. But until then we have to play the way we do play it.

But we were at the time attempting to put ourselves in a state of readiness to make an assault on the state. It's no secret we were accumulating weapons. We were accumulating equipment of various kinds, and a certain amount of that was coming from the military. But you know, whenever someone is about to make a gift to you of a Beretta or something like that you can't send someone to collect it. This is what C. L. R. was attempting to say, that "why were we there? What was Walter doing there? You don't send generals out in the field to do this kind of work. Why wasn't it someone else?" Well, he says, "Perhaps the reason was that Walter had to show he was not asking people to do something he wouldn't do himself." Well, that was part of it, but not the whole thing. The real thing was nobody would hand over their weapon to a messenger. They would hand it over to me, to Walter, or one of the leaders; they would not give it to anybody less, because of the fact that Burnham had penetrated so much of the WPA, which they knew and it was a very dangerous game we were playing. In point of fact, we found ourselves at all hours of the night, in strange places, doing dangerous things because those were the things that were necessary to do, it seemed to us at that time. The miracle is that more of us didn't get killed.

But to come back to some of the things we talked about earlier. I didn't have the advantage of knowing Walter very well at school. He was a year ahead of me. He had, in fact, belonged to the first batch of working-class youth who benefited from the PPP educational scholarship program. In those days, government county scholarships had been initiated by the first PPP government of 1953. Walter belonged to the first batch of students who benefited from that. I belonged to the second, and so you knew that ahead of you were these extraordinary people. He was one of them. You could not be at Queen's, at the time, and not know of his skills at debating, his activities on the sports field, and his academics. As you know, Queen's in those days, not so much now, but in those days certainly it was a kind of thoroughbred place. It had different rules for thoroughbreds and different rules for cart horses, or who they identified as cart horses.

Many of these people identified as cart horses turned out to be extremely accomplished people in later life. I remember sometime in later life when I came across someone I knew to have been designated a cart horse but was now doing something extraordinary in the world. I said to myself, "Wasn't this the guy who was a cart horse when we were at school?" Of course, because it was that kind of school; it was rigidly hierarchical and stratified. Walter was among the stars of the school.

I remember when UWI initiated its open scholarship, one of which Walter was to win. Queen's won most of them and it caused some consternation in CARICOM[7] because one has to share these things in the region. You could not be giving them all to one school, which is essentially how it ended up being. You had people like Ewart Thomas.[8] I don't think Ewart Thomas ever lost a mark in a mathematics exam, as far as I recall. These were the days when they would do pure math in the lower sixth. It was really fairly normal for them to score a hundred in these mathematics exams. We had a very powerful math department.

I didn't know Walter all that well at school. He went off to UWI.[9] He went off to Jamaica. It was not until I was in Cambridge—I had gone off to St. John's, I was an undergraduate up there; he had by this time gone up to SOAS[10]—that we really established contact again. Ewart Thomas was also at Cambridge. He and Ewart were, of course, contemporaries, and close. I remember he and Ewart visiting my room in Cambridge, and we had an easy traffic of ideas and discussions. But I became much closer to him later on when I was at Cornell. I had done my graduate work at Cornell. I stayed on after I graduated. I was teaching comparative literature. He was a visiting Professor of African Studies attached to the Ujamaa Center. He used to come annually, I believe.

There was a particular context the last time I saw him at Cornell, which was when we ourselves were caught up in a huge struggle on campus related to some issues dealing with minority students. It was a period of great turmoil. You know what North American campuses were like in this period. In fact, my real attraction to Cornell was—I don't know if you remember the *Time* magazine cover that showed this African brother with bullets across his chest standing outside of Willard Straight Hall with an AK-47 in his hand?[11] This was very much the tone of the campuses of the time. I was attracted to Cornell because of its militancy and its history of traditions. I remember Walter coming to one of my reading groups. We were reading Hegel or something ambitious. He came, sat around, talked, and he participated in the group. It was at this time that he began to really talk to me seriously about coming back to Guyana.

I had not given any thought to going back to Guyana. I had become so disenchanted with what had happened in Guyana in the 1960s. When I left there in 1962, February, it happened, the burning of the city. That was the very year I was doing the Guyana scholarship.[12] Literally, the town was burning, and we were attempting to work. When I left in 1962, I did not even wait for exam results to leave. I left even before the exam results came out. I had been fairly active politically. I had grown up around the PPP. My parents were both members of the PPP. My father was a member of the General Council. Walter also had PPP attachments,[13] and what else was one to be in those days? It was the progressive movement, anti-colonial.

The whole tenor of the time, the issues at Cornell, my own—I think of it as "edginess at Ithaca." I had, a couple of years before, gone to Portugal on my study leave and had been on the streets of Lisbon during the time of the Portuguese revolution in 1974, which was the year. In the summer of that year they had the most progressive government in Portugal. They had many, as you know. The sixth government was the government of Vasco Gonçalves.[14] In that period the book that was in all the bookshops in Lisbon was the Portuguese translation of *How Europe Underdeveloped Africa*. It was the period when they were talking about the Africanization of the Portuguese revolution. The Portuguese armies that went to Mozambique and Angola to fight against the African liberation fighters came back completely infected by the guerilla movement. They came back and overthrew Caetano, but were themselves under attack from the right.

The success of the Portuguese revolution had to do with a number of things. Like COPCON, which was an internal military unit, a unit of the army led by a man called General Otelo.[15] Otelo was very close to Fidel and close to Cuba. Then, of course, there was all this Africanization. And then Walter's book—it was the first time I had seen it in Portuguese translation and it was literally in all the bookshops in Lisbon. It was the book of the summer. I left Lisbon and went back to Ithaca. I can tell you, to leave revolutionary Lisbon and go back to upstate New York was a bit of a culture shock. I began to get very edgy at Cornell and felt that I had come to the end of my usefulness in the States. Really, I could not see myself becoming a tenured academic professor in an American university. I was really looking for options at that time.

I had serious thoughts about Mozambique, because I had met a number of comrades in Lisbon from Mozambique. They talked to me about going to a university there, and I was also pursuing the possibility of going to Havana. It was just at this time that Walter came. We renewed contact. Then he began to talk to me about what was happening in Guyana, something to which I had not given much thought, largely because of what had happened. I felt that the way in which Guyana had developed in the 1960s, what had happened then, really removed any possibility of progressive politics that was non-racial. And since I have no particular ethnic reflexes, have no interest in anything like that, I didn't see any room. People are often surprised when I tell them I participated in my first election campaign in 1961. As a boy, I was distributing election flyers for the PPP in those days. So I grew up in a very political household and was political all my life.

So when in 1975, '76, Walter was talking to me about the WPA and what they were able to achieve, what had happened in that period, the work Eusi Kwayana, Moses Bhagwan, and Clive Thomas were doing, I felt that there was a real possibility, that space was opening up. There was a real movement. Walter really persuaded me to come home and I did. I took the decision; we came home and I came home with a film project.[16] The idea was that I would come and we would try to do this film as a way of reentering the society. I did not apply to the university for a job since I felt I was coming back to Guyana and this was home, and I didn't think it was necessary for me to be doing things like that.

Eventually, when I got here, I did apply to the University of Guyana. But I believe because of some security concerns that I was only appointed in February of 1977. I missed the entire first part of the year and eventually joined the university in 1977. At that time, I was becoming more and more involved in the WPA movement and WPA politics and became closer and closer to Walter. So our closest time, actually, as friends, as comrades, was in the period when I was here in Guyana and with the WPA.

Although we had played cards before, we didn't play cards as intensely as we played them in that period. Because frequently we would have to leave the tenseness of the street and the difficulties of public meetings. In some of those early public meetings of the WPA, Walter and I would spend the afternoon advertising the meetings, and then we would go and set up the microphones, then we would speak at the meetings, then we would dismantle the system, the speakers, and take them home. So it was a period of extremely intense activity, some of it dangerous, and then we would go to the Bridge Club in Georgetown.

I have never known a more dogmatic bridge player than Walter Rodney. He never made any mistakes. "Only authors made mistakes," he said. He was always extremely certain of everything. In fact, he had come upon a system, which apparently had been drawn up somewhere, and he gave me a copy and said we had to master this system. I tried to tell him, "Walter, you know it's not possible in competitive bridge to have secret systems. One has to declare to people what these systems mean." He saw that. He wasn't trying to get ahead of anybody with a fast one. But the system was so complex. Anyway, we played a lot. In fact, one of the more moving tributes, in a small way, which is not known very much, is that on the night of the assassination, the Guyana Bridge Club stood for a moment of silence to mark his death. People were very fond of him. He was a person very easy to be fond of: instinctively charming, simple.

I remember once when I took Deryck Murray,[17] a very, very close friend of mine, to meet Walter. We had played cricket at Cambridge together, Deryck and I, and he was here with the West Indies team.

Walter, of course, was delighted to meet Deryck. Cricket, this was another great passion of his. So I took Deryck to South[18] to meet Walter. We chatted. Walter talked a lot about cricket. When we left, driving back, Deryck said, "You know, I'm completely amazed. What an extremely simple brother this is, man." This was one of Walter's marks. He is one of those people who can appeal instantly to people. There are people in life you meet for the first time and you feel you have known them for a long time. He was one of those human beings who had a very instinctive contact with persons in all walks of life. Walter can have that impression on prime ministers and bauxite workers as well. There was no difficulty on his part. He had a biology completely open to persons, which, of course, was part of his undoing.

One of the things that made life very difficult working with Walter was that Walter believed that any black man who came to him and said that he had broken with Burnham, was prepared to fight Burnham, should be welcomed. Walter embraced them. Of course, this was in that period when Burnham was sending us agents, infiltrating the party, and so on. It was very dangerous. In a real sense, Walter had to be protected against his own generosity, his own openness.

I never met Mr. Gregory Smith[19] at all, never met him. But I understand that he would visit Walter's house and that kind of thing. I can see that Walter, having decided that Gregory Smith was of some use to the movement, would also have treated him like a brother, brought him into his home, met his children, and that kind of thing. I never once met the man. We had had a couple of assassinations. Ohene Koama[20] had been shot down in South. Dublin[21] had been killed on the streets by the police in Linden. After these things happened, we instituted some special security procedures in the party. One of them was that anybody we were recruiting from the military would pass through a special security body that was made up of ex-military captains and officers who would know everyone. So it was really a way of passing them through a security sieve, as it were. Gregory Smith's name was never brought to the committee.

This was always, to me, a very strange, strange thing. This entire dispute about whether he was struck off active duty, or whether he was still on or whether he was an agent, and all of that, I feel all this could have been revealed in the course of the kind of investigation that would have taken place.

Although, as I have said to some people who accused us of recklessness—it's one of the points I made about the C. L. R. interview—you know when the state decides to take you out; if they miss taking you out on Friday, they'll take you out on Saturday. If they don't take you out on Saturday, they'll take you out a month from now. Once the state makes that decision, it's very difficult, how you can secure yourself. What are you going to do? No number of bodyguards, no number, or how much precaution you take. I mean, I think once that decision is taken at that kind of level, that's it. You either go into exile, which of course many people asked Walter to do. And as you know Mugabe, when he went to Zimbabwe, asked him to stay in Zimbabwe and write a history of Zimbabwe. A lot of his friends asked, "Why are you going back there [to Guyana]?" They saw where this was heading. Perhaps Walter had an inkling of where it was heading as well. But he clearly felt, at that time, firmly committed to what it is he was doing. But those were the issues and those were the difficulties.

I think that not enough has been done, not enough study, on the currents at work during the 1978, '79, '80 period. This is something that still needs to be worked through. Part of the reason it cannot be totally understood is because, of course, not everything can be revealed. We are still in a position where only so much can be revealed about the period. Until we get either some truth commission or commission of enquiry, where all the parties come to the table and are prepared to say what it is they did, it's always going to be incomplete.

Contrary to Ricky Singh's[22] accusations of betrayal, when Pat Rodney[23] came here and talked about wanting a commission of enquiry of a certain kind, she made it very clear what kind of commission she wanted. She was interested in some kind of reconciliation.

That's what she was interested in. She was not interested in vengeance. She was not interested in any of those things. She really was interested in the kind of commission that could lead to some reconciliation in Guyana. It seemed to me that the best way to get this was to have a motion that could be, in effect, unanimously adopted by the National Assembly. The first copy of the motion I saw, which was the first copy circulated by the government, was not a motion that was going to be agreed on by the PNC. It was not. I felt it was more important to win the support of the entire parliament than, once again, using the motion as a stick to beat the PNC with. Bear in mind, that the PNC that we are dealing with in 2006, 2007, most of these people have no idea of what we are talking about. These are young people. They had nothing to do with 1980. Most of them were children. Some of them were not even born.

I had much to do with winning support for the motion, and I took a copy of the amended motion to the government side, tried to sell it to them with my reasoning of the time. I then took it to the PNC and said this is what we want you to agree to, and effectively moving as I did between the two sides, I arrived at a form of words that could have been supported by both sides in the parliament. The one thing we did not want the commission of enquiry to become was a slugging match between the PPP and PNC. It was part of the reason why, during the buildup to the last election, we deliberately said quite openly we had no interest in the commission of enquiry being caught up in the election abuse and slander that was going on. This is not what we wanted. We had waited thirty years for this enquiry and, frankly, waiting another three years is not going to affect very much. What we did not want—remember at the time the PPP was very gung-ho to get the enquiry because they really wanted it as a stick to beat the PNC before the election—was Walter to be used by the PPP in this way. So, as I said, this was the main reason for moving to that form of words.

The problem with Rickey is, and I don't often say much about it, but to my mind Rickey has yet to come out with a single article that recognizes and condemns the rampant corruption in the PPP, the racism in the PPP, the authoritarianism in the PPP. Where is Rickey's voice? Rickey was a strong voice when he was fighting all these things in the PNC. Many people living in Guyana will tell you that today these things are, in fact, much worse. It is worse in the sense that the velocity of corruption is such that it is quite extraordinary. It is quite extraordinary what has happened here. The arrival of organized crime, the involvement of high figures in the government in the international narcotics industry, and so on, these are extraordinary happenings. I see not a whimper from Rickey Singh about any of this. I think that he has, for people like me, lost a lot of his credibility as a journalist. I think his creed, at the time of the motion, was very much part of the PPP. The PPP was on to that, too; the WPA has betrayed Walter and this and that. He was joining that chorus. I frankly didn't take it very seriously.

But, back to Walter, he loved cricket. He knew I played for Cambridge. But I don't think he did very much. He had the strangest action as a bowler.[24] He might have played for his house,[25] or something. But cricket was a passion in the sense that he knew everything there was to know about it. He was a keen student of the game, but was not himself a performer. He did not write on it, though a passionate devotee of the game. What he excelled in at school was athletics. He was a high jumper. He was a fine athlete. And, of course, we attempted to be complete persons at school. In those days, we didn't see any great conflict in excelling academically and excelling at sports or going to parties. We lived quite fully. These days when I see these poor children traipsing off to extra lessons, I think to myself, I don't know where I would have found the time for extra lessons, because of the fullness of our lives at school. Walter led an extremely full life at school. He was an absolutely outstanding academic. He was a debater of rare quality. He was a sportsperson. He partied with the best of them. He was quite a dancer.

About his death, boy! It was a long time before I felt anything. I think what I felt on the night of June thirteenth was mostly numbness. Because I had the very thankless task of actually going around and notifying the members of the executive of what had happened.

As you can imagine, the streets were extremely tense. Andaiye[26] and Karen[27] were in the face of the horror. I had seen what had happened. I raced out to the East Coast to alert Kwayana. I had to go up to Buxton. I remember going to Better Hope[28] where Moses lived at the time. I went around and saw all the members of the leadership of the party to convene an immediate emergency meeting to discuss what had happened. Then I was caught up for days after that dealing with the details of what had happened, cleaning out the houses that might be searched, dealing with the body, dealing with the pathologist, all these things. In fact, I felt years after that perhaps—I had been very close to Pat and the children over the years—one of the things that caused some distance between us for some time was that I was not there in the house with them enough following the assassination. Because of all the people they would have expected to be there, I would have been there. But I was really caught up with the practical logistical things that had to be done. It took some time for what had happened to affect me emotionally. All I can say is that it is something that affects me up to now. I have moments when I think of Walter.

My own son, who was very small at the time, ten, eleven years old, had spent some time in Guyana as a child and was very close to Walter. I hadn't even realized how close he had gotten to Walter. But Walter was one of those people who children felt comfortable with. He obviously felt closer to Walter than to some of the other comrades in the party. He was living in Jamaica with his mother when the assassination happened. His mother told me, subsequently, that he did not speak to anyone for four days, did not utter a word. So I think a lot of people responded in their particular ways. I confessed to not having that kind of emotional response. I had to give the main WPA address at the funeral. We were busy making security arrangements. It was really a hell of a time. In a real sense, I actually shut out that aspect of things and put it aside so I could do the things that had to be done. The price I paid for doing that is that it has continued to affect me all through the years.

When I went to the C. L. R. James lecture in Trinidad,[29] and felt the need to go back to that, go over that, and to let the comrades in

Trinidad know far more about the environment, the circumstances, what was on the ground, what was really at play, to give them a fuller understanding and to make sense of C. L. R.'s cry of pain. I continue to believe that was a cry of pain in that essay more than anything else. So, in a very real sense, I think that is how a number of us registered this particular loss.

I saw someone writing even today that had Walter not been killed, the WPA would be ruling Guyana. I am not quite as confident of that as the journalist who wrote it. Of course, a number of people say that after Walter died, the movement died. Well, the movement didn't die. It could not be the same. How could you lose a Walter Rodney and not be weakened? But after Walter died in 1980, we contested the elections of 1985. We did far better than the results ever showed. When Walter was there fighting during the period of civil rebellion, we were organized, mostly in Georgetown, in Linden, very little organization in the villages, and no organization at all in the Sugar Belt. Because in those days, working very closely with the PPP, we had accepted this territorial division of the country, where we would not go and try to organize among the sugar workers. Again, this was during the time of the rebellion. Of course, subsequently we had to do it. But I think that the loss for the nation and part of the ongoing tragedy is that there is so much ignorance in the country, so you talk to young people in the country. During the twenty-fifth anniversary commemoration of Walter's death, people went to schools and talked to schoolchildren and it was amazing how little was known by people who ought to know. Why doesn't the Ministry of Education have material on Walter's work and life in the schools so that our children can grow up knowing about him? They are the best people to explain that. But, to my mind, not to hold up this example to the young people of this country, especially in a season of such degeneration and degradation, not to hold up this light, to them, is to be participating in that degradation: keeping people at the necessary levels you need to control them. I see no reason why such an astonishing example of everything that is best should not be inspiring the minds of the young.

His scholarship was far-reaching. I was in Uganda fairly recently, and, of course, that was a place he had many friends, among them Museveni[30] himself, and many comrades in the movement at the time. In fact, Museveni was one of Walter's keener students when he was at the university. I know that in Tanzania *How Europe Underdeveloped Africa* is still a book in the hands of young people and is being studied in the universities. An extraordinary influence in terms of the development of Africa's historiography. There were many people working in that direction. He was not a complete pioneer, but the work he did in that area, to see Africa anew, differently, was really an outstanding, outstanding achievement—and for one so young. Walter was thirty-eight when he died. When you think of what was achieved in that short life. The young people of Africa, the Caribbean, Jamaica, the Black Power movement—I don't know if we would have seen the NJM[31] and NJAC,[32] and all of these movements that came up in the period, were it not for the Rodney Riots in Jamaica and his extraordinary influence among the Rastafari.

He was not only a profound political influence, he was a deep cultural influence as well. Of course, he had taught in the United States. So many people as far away as California, New York, and so on would know of his work. There are many people who today would proudly declare themselves to be Rodneyists. I think of the work people like Horace Campbell[33] are doing, Winston James,[34] and a number of people across the world, young scholars and some not so young, who are carrying on that legacy of committed scholarship. Walter's scholarship was, in the first instance, really a scholarship about changing the world. It was not a scholarship about footnotes, tenure: it was a scholarship about changing the world. That to my mind is its enduring value.

CONTRIBUTORS

AMIRI BARAKA is a noted poet, novelist, critic, and playwright, Baraka was born and still lives in Newark, New Jersey. Founder of the Harlem-based Black Arts Movement, now defunct, he has published many books and continues to teach, write, and protest. He is one of the foremost writers and thinkers of this century. He served as Poet Laureate of New Jersey before his untimely and unceremonious removal from the position following publication of his poem "Who Blew Up America."

ABBYSSINIAN CARTO is a graphic artist working and living in Brooklyn, New York. Carto continues to exhibit and remains committed to the upliftment of the region and equal rights for all. A graduate of the City University of New York, Carto participated in the struggle and civil rebellion during that crucial period in Guyana from 1979 to 1980 and has the scars to show for it.

BRENDA DO HARRIS teaches at Bowie State University in Maryland and has published two novels rooted in her Guyanese experience: *The Coloured Girl in the Ring: A Guyanese Woman Remembers* and *Calabash Parkway: A Novel*. The latter is set in Brooklyn, New York.

ROBERT HILL was most recently a professor of history at UCLA and archivist for the Marcus Garvey papers. Hill was part of the early Institute of the Black World (IBW) in Atlanta, which included Manning Marable, Bill Strickland, and Howard Dodson, among others. The IBW was an important stop on Rodney's continuous lecture tour, and where Hill reconnected with Rodney, whom he had accompanied in 1968 to the Black Writers' Congress in Montreal.

ROBERT "BOBBY" MOORE taught Walter Rodney in high school and is credited with pointing Rodney to the study of history. An early graduate of the University College of the West Indies, Moore shared the legacy of another distinguished historian, Elsa Goveia, with his young charges at Queen's College through the notes he took in Goveia's classes at UWI. He also served as Guyana's Consular General to Canada, where he currently resides. Rodney also studied under Goveia at UWI.

LEITH MULLINGS is Distinguished Professor of Anthropology at City University of New York, Graduate Center; she has taught at several universities including Yale. She co-edited an anthology of African American history with her husband, the late Manning Marable, *Let No One Turn Us Around* (New York: Rowan and Littlefield, 2003).

RUPERT ROOPNARAINE is one of the founding leaders of the Working People's Alliance (WPA). Roopnaraine is currently a member of Guyana's parliament, representing a coalition that includes the WPA, People's National Congress, and others. He has taught at several universities, including Cornell and the University of Guyana.

ISSA G. SHIVJI was born in Tanzania. Dr. Shivji is currently the Mwalimu Julius Nyerere Chair at the University of Dar Es Salaam. Part of the mandate of the chair is to reenergize the debates that characterized the university during the time of Julius Nyerere's presidency and Rodney's stay. Dr. Shivji continues to write and host the annual Mwalimu Julius Nyerere Intellectual Festival.

CLIVE YOLANDE THOMAS is a distinguished economist and a prolific writer on globalization as it applies to developing nations and the Caribbean in particular. He is in demand as a consultant on economic policy. Some of his volumes include *Dependence and Transformation: The Economics of the Transition to Socialism* (New York: Monthly Review Press, 1976); and *The Rise of the Authoritarian State in Peripheral Societies* (Portsmouth, NH: Heinemann, 1984).

NOTES

INTRODUCTION / 1—CLAIRMONT CHUNG

1. Born on the Caribbean island of Martinique, Frantz Fanon left his home to avoid conscription into the forces loyal to Adolf Hitler. He reached France and there qualified as a psychiatrist. He wrote several books, including his best-known, *The Wretched of the Earth*, which deals with the struggle for liberation from colonial domination and the role of armed struggle as more than justified where arms protect colonial power. *Black Skin, White Masks,* trans. Charles Lam Markmann (1967; repr.,New York: Grove Press, 1952); *The Wretched of the Earth*, trans. Constance Farrington (1963; repr., New York: Grove Weidenfeld, 1961).

2. Mao Zedong (Mao Tse-tung) is credited with spearheading China's Cultural Revolution and was a favorite of the socialist and socialist-leaning Black Power activists. His goal was to purge China of capitalist-inspired elements, and this included people, institutions, and culture. Some of it was bloody.

3. In 1966, Bobby Seale cofounded the Black Panther Party with Huey Newton.

4. H. Rap Brown is currently in jail for life under his Muslim name, Jamil Abdullah al-Amin, for the killing of a Fulton County, Georgia, Sheriff's deputy and the wounding of another. He was chairman of the Student Nonviolent Coordinating Committee (SNCC) and briefly served as the minister of justice in the Black Panther Party. He was hounded by the FBI and spent significant time in prison as a result. His biography, *Die Nigger Die*, was a popular read during that period.

5. George Jackson, Fleeta Drumgo, and John Clutchette would become the "Soledad Brothers" during their trial for the death of a prison guard while serving time in Soledad Prison in California. The guard's death was supposedly in retaliation for the deaths of three black prisoners killed by a guard sniper during a prison fight three days earlier. Jackson was allegedly killed in a shootout in prison during an attempt to escape. His book, *Blood in My Eye,* was compulsory reading for revolutionaries.

6. Here Walter Rodney described George Jackson's commitment to the struggle, his understanding of capitalism, and by extension the Marxist analysis employed by the Black Panther Party. Jackson was to clarify his own positions in his book *Blood in My Eye* (New York: Random House, 1971, published posthumously).

7. In *Blood in My Eye*, Jackson talks about the study of Mao, Lenin, Trotsky, and Marx in prison.

8. The People's National Congress, founded and led by Forbes Burnham until his death in 1985, presided over the country using a doctrine of party paramountcy. PNC thus controlled all state institutions and distributed those resources based on loyalty to the party: a kind of official state-sanctioned corruption.

9. The People's Progressive Party began the formal political struggle for voting rights and independence. Cheddi Jagan and Forbes Burnham have come to characterize the leading factions within the PPP, that is, until the split in 1955. By 1953 increased participation led to seats in the Legislative Council sufficient to introduce a new constitution. However, that constitution and pro working-class initiatives resulted in an invasion by Britain and the suspension of the constitution. Since the country was a British colony at the time, "invasion" may not be the correct legal term, but in practice it was an invasion.

10. On February 21, 1965, Malcolm X, El Hajj Malik El Shabazz, was assassinated in New York City. Malcolm X remains arguably the most important contributor to the Black Power movement and a leading figure in American history.

11. Dr. Martin Luther King Jr. was assassinated on April 4, 1968.

12. The president of the United States, John F. Kennedy, was assassinated on November 22, 1963, and his brother Robert Kennedy, former U.S. attorney general, was assassinated while campaigning for the presidency on June 6, 1968.

13. In 1969, students at Sir George William University in Montreal, since renamed Concordia University, took over a computer room in protest against a racially biased faculty member. Security forces stormed the room after two weeks, but not before the students threw the equipment out the window. Commentators have credited the Congress of Black Writers for creating the climate that would lead to a student takeover. A number of

students were charged and tried. The results of the trials led to protest in an already protest-ready Caribbean. Its greatest effect was felt in Trinidad and Tobago, and the Black Power movement there, led by the National Joint Action Committee, took up the cause. The mutiny followed.

14. On April 21, 1970, a section of the Trinidad and Tobago Regiment refused orders to shoot civilians during the state of emergency declared in response to ongoing protest in solidarity with the Montreal students, who were mostly Caribbean. This is referred to as "the mutiny." Led by Lieutenants Raffique Shah and Rex LaSalle, the mutineers made an attempt to march on the capital, Port of Spain, but were turned back by attacks from the local navy, the threat of greater bloodshed, the arrival of U.S. Navy vessels, and their implications. A court-martial ensued.

15. On hearing of Rodney's exclusion, UWI students planned a protest march, which escalated into a full-scale battle between the state and elements opposed to it and its decision to exclude Rodney. It resulted in three reported deaths, millions of dollars in property damage, and energized the entire country, perhaps the region, in a movement for civil rights and real independence.

16. The Hyde Park, London, "soapbox" from which various speakers shared their views was actually a four-foot ladder that the speaker would climb to deliver his or her speech. Rodney would use this ladder technique to test his views and hone his oratory.

17. Davis was a popular community activist and speaker on issues in the black community.

18. Dr. Ben-Jochannan was an expert on Nile Valley civilizations and author of numerous books.

19. Elombe Brath served as a graphics artist for WABC-TV's Gil Noble–hosted *Like It Is*, a weekly magazine show that concentrated on issues affecting Africa and its diaspora. Brath is a noted activist with formidable amounts of knowledge on African affairs.

20. University on the Corner of Lenox Avenue (UCLA) was used to describe the whole street education culture of Harlem, of which Liberation Bookstore took a central spot at 131st Street and Lenox Avenue. Its proprietrix, Una Mulzac, had traveled to British Guiana during the violence of the 1960s with the hope of helping the progressive forces, but was injured by a mail bomb that also killed Michael Forde, a PPP activist after whom the party named a local bookstore. She returned to the United States and subsequently opened a bookstore.

21. Guyana-born professor and writer on the African presence in antiquity and particularly on the presence of Africans in the Americas before Columbus.

22. Trinidadian professor and author, considered an authority on Marcus Garvey.

23. Edward Scobie, a native of Dominica, wrote on the presence of Africans in ancient Europe. At the time of his death in 1996, Dr. Scobie was Professor Emeritus of History, Black Studies Department, City College of New York.

24. Dr. Leonard Jeffries headed the Black Studies Department at City College of New York.

25. In 1763, Cuffy led a successful revolution against the Dutch slaveholders of Berbice, then a Dutch colony. The rebels drove the Dutch from their seat of power at Fort Nassau and down the Berbice River. The Dutch regrouped and retook the river after a year, only to later lose Berbice to the British. Berbice became the easternmost county of Guyana.

26. Toussaint L'Ouverture led the Haitian Revolution against the French, a story fictionalized in *The Black Jacobins*, a novel by C. L. R. James.

27. "Redemption Song," lyrics by Robert Marley.

28. C. L. R. James, *Walter Rodney and the Question of Power* (London: Race Today Publications, 1981).

29. Scholars do not all agree on the dates of the period of Enlightenment, but most agree it includes the hundred years beginning around 1730 and ending around 1830. It was during this time that the writings of philosophers like Diderot, Rousseau, Voltaire, and Pascal were used as references to engage in the then-new ideas of inclusion and civil rights. Many of the Pan-Africanist scholars named here, like Jeffries and Van Sertima, disagree, and point to European contact with Africa as the beginning of Europe's Enlightenment period.

30. Independence negotiated in the capital cities like London and Paris, as opposed to the bush of Berbice.

31. In his letters, Cuffy signed his title as "Governor of the Negroes of Berbice." Some interpreted that as leaving space for a white governor like Hoogenheim or at a minimum evoking the sense of equality. Hoogenheim served as governor of Berbice, but it's important to note that he was not a representative of the Dutch monarchy; instead he worked for the Dutch West India Company, which resembled, in form, the corporations we know today with boards of directors and investors. However, he enjoyed the full protection of Dutch military forces.

32. George Pinckard, *Letters from Guiana*, taken from *Notes on the West Indies . . . and the coast of Guiana, 1796–1797*, reprinted in *Guiana Chronicle*, 1942, Georgetown *(Guiana Edition No. 5)* and cited in Vere T. Daly, *A Short History of the Guyanese People* (London: Macmillan Educational, 1975).

33. A study group headed by noted historian, activist, Marxist, and philosopher C. L. R. James included Rodney, Richard Small, Selma James, Jessica Huntley, Eric Huntley, and many others. Richard Small later formed the legal team that defended Rodney during his treason

trial in Guyana. The Huntleys, along with Richard Small, started Bogle L'Ouverture Publishing, and their first book was Walter Rodney's *The Groundings with My Brothers*.

34. Many, including Herman Ferguson, a witness to Malcolm X's murder, fled to Guyana to avoid prosecution for activities associated with the two organizations Malcolm X founded: Organization of Afro-American Unity (OAAU) and Muslim Mosque, Inc. (MMI). James 67X, Abdul Razzaq, another eyewitness to Malcolm's murder, sought refuge in Guyana. Both men lived there for close to twenty years but are now back in the United States. It was another American "fugitive," David Hill, known as Rabbi Washington, who terrorized anti-government protesters and contributed to the climate that would lead to Rodney's assassination in Guyana.

35. A "rude-boy" or "rudie" is one who subscribed to a counterculture that was popularized by the youth of that period who sought new ways of expression against the status quo. They walked and talked a certain way. They had their own music. The current equivalent would be the hip-hop culture. A true rudie never really becomes anything else, irrespective of his or her vocation.

36. The Occupy Wall Street (OWS) movement began actual occupation of Liberty Park in downtown New York City on September 17, 2011. Its message targeted the banks and their control over government and against people. People from all over the United States came to New York to show support, and to take the message back. Similar actions began in most major American cities and spread across the world.

37. The Dutch West India Company had a charter to develop lands in the New World. New York City was once New Amsterdam; the capital of Berbice is New Amsterdam. The Dutch West India Company brought captured Africans to New York and to Berbice. They operated in much the same way as the corporations now challenged by the Occupy Wall Street movement.

38. Walter Rodney, *The Groundings with My Brothers* (Chicago: Frontline Distribution International, 1969).

39. *Tahrir* translated from Arabic means "freedom" and is the name of the square from which the protest made its most public expression. It has become a symbol for protest everywhere. Many have died and more injured in Tahrir Square, with no sign of let up.

2—ROBERT "BOBBY" MOORE / Ottawa, 2010

1. The Dissertation was published as *A History of the Upper Guinea Coast, 1545–1800* (Oxford: Oxford University Press, 1970), later reprinted by Clarendon Press and Monthly Review Press. *How Europe Underdevloped*

Africa (Washington, D.C.: Howard University Press, 1972).

2. Classical meant the student intended to focus on areas outside the traditional sciences and would study languages and social science.

3. Trevor Huddleston, *Naught for Your Comfort* (New York: Doubleday, 1956).

3 —ABYSSINIAN CARTO / Brooklyn, 2007

1. Hernán Cortés and his Spanish flotilla arrived off the coast of Mexico in the spring of 1519 and proceeded to lead one of the bloodiest episodes of European conquests of native peoples in the history of the Western world.

2   Cesar Estrada Chávez was an iconic figure in the American labor movement and to farm workers in particular. Chávez cofounded the National Farm Workers Association, which became the United Farm Workers and used civil disobedience to bring attention to the plight of farm workers everywhere.

3. Forbes Burnham formed the People's National Congress in 1955 and became premier in 1964 as a result of a coalition with United Force, a conservative party, and assistance from both the United States and Britain. Independence from Britain followed in 1966, and Forbes Burnham ruled in one capacity as premier, prime minister, and president until his death in 1985.

4. Tiger Bay is a port community officially known as South Cummingsburg that received its unofficial name because of its similarities to the notorious port area of the same name in Glasgow, Scotland. It's a community of the poorest residents of the city living in mostly condemned or ought-to-be-condemned housing bordered by some of the more prominent businesses in the country.

5. In 1963, the People's National Congress (PNC), with a predominantly African membership and led by Forbes Burnham, needed the help of the predominantly Portuguese business class and their party, United Force, to win the election of 1964. That coalition was forged with the help of the CIA, whose funds supported an eighty-day general strike. Employees as well as employers joined the strike. Violence marred the period leading up to the election.

6. The United Force (UF) was a party led by businessman Peter D'Aguiar who supported the capitalist policies of U.S. interests.

7. In 1973, at the ruling PNC's conference, the *Declaration of Sophia* was unveiled by Forbes Burnham. This was an adapted socialist manifesto similar to the *Arusha Declaration* of Tanzania's Julius Nyerere. Part of that declaration was a national referendum that would lead to a change in the

country's constitution and elevate the Party as the paramount political organization.

8. The People's Progressive Party grew out of the anti-colonial struggle and began as a multiracial party that included Forbes Burnham and Cheddi Jagan. In 1953, it came to power at the first elections with full adult suffrage. In 1955, Burnham split from the PPP and formed the PNC.

9. "Liming," a Caribbean term, originally meant men standing, hanging around, on the street corner in conversation, perhaps like a lime on a tree. The term dates back to the early work stoppages of the anti-slavery and labor movement. It has evolved to mean almost any gathering of all sexes not involved in work for pay and sometimes liming is engaged in even during work for pay.

10. The Ministry of National Development also served the Congress Place headquarters of the ruling PNC and a symbol of the merger between the party and the state; Party Paramountcy.

11. Both Omowale and Rupert Roopnaraine were senior members of the Working People's Alliance and lecturers at the University of Guyana. Roopnaraine's interview appears in this volume.

12. Martin Carter served as a poetic voice of the people. He authored several volumes of poetry including the popular *Poems of Resistance*.

13. The House of Israel is a church headed by an American fugitive, David Hill, known as Rabbi Washington. Members were used by the PNC government to commit acts of terror against dissenters.

14. Meetings are public fora held by a political party as a way of communicating its ideas. It's a tradition in Guyana and predates the introduction of television.

15. Nigel Westmaas, a WPA activist, was pursued into a cane field by state agents and hid overnight in the field to avoid capture.

16. An open area, a promenade between two canals, used for recreation and historically the site of political meetings. A portion of it now houses an extension from Bourda Market.

17. Most likely referring to Martin Carter's *Poems of Resistance*, (1954), "Death of a Comrade":

> Death must not find us thinking that we die.
> Too soon, too soon
> our banner draped for you.
> I would prefer
> the banner in the wind
> Not bound so tightly

18. The Mall best resembles a public park and historically used for political meetings.

19. Tall, slimly built, and light-skinned. "Red" covers a wide swath of skin colors that range from near-white to brown, but generally means a lighter shade of brown.

20. The Demerara River runs 345 kilometers from its source to its mouth at the Atlantic Ocean where the capital city, Georgetown, sits.

21. Walter Rodney, *AHistory of the Guyanese Working People, 1881–1905* (Baltimore: Johns Hopkins University Press, 1981).

22. Donald is Walter's brother and was in the car with Walter when the bomb exploded.

23. Andaiye is Abbyssinian's sister and Karen DeSouza is a friend. The three, all members of the WPA, shared a flat. DeSouza was arrested along with other leaders in the aftermath of the burning of the Ministry of National Development.

24. It has been suggested that Smith's intent was to lure Walter close to the prison so that when the bomb exploded, the government would then be able to say that Rodney was attempting to blow up the prison. David Hinds, one of the WPA activists, was at the same time being held in the prison for a weapons offense.

25. The opposite of the Midas touch as articulated by Rodney was that everything Burnham touched turned to shit. The mythical King Midas turned everything he touched into gold.

26. Burnham's sister, Jessie Burnham, published a pamphlet warning of her brother's singular desire for power titled *Beware of My Brother Forbes* (1964).

27. The twenty-fifth anniversary of Walter Rodney's assassination was commemorated with a series of activities that drew many of his colleagues to Guyana in 2005.

28. Michael Manley and Errol Barrow, former prime ministers of Jamaica and Barbados, respectively, hold similar positions in their country's histories as Burnham. They were not identified with the kind of repression experienced in Guyana but were important parts of their countries' transformation from under colonial rule.

29. The writer is an artist and for part of that 1978–1979 period had taught graphic design at the E. R. Burrows School of Art in Georgetown, Guyana.

30. Bishops' High School and Queen's College were girls' and boys' schools, respectively, and were attended mostly by children of the upper-middle and upper classes, and aspirants to those classes. According to his sister, Burnham transferred from Central High School to Queen's College after a few incidents with students taking advantage of his small size.

4—DR. BRENDA DO HARRIS / Bowie, Maryland, August 2007

1. Guyana National Service was a paramilitary organization formed to aid in national development projects and provide opportunities to youth in skills training, and many benefited from it. However, National Service became a de facto prerequisite for securing government-sponsored scholarships.

2. Eusi Kwayana, a political activist since the 1940s, helped found and develop the African Society for Cultural Relations with Independent Africa (ASCRIA). This organization later merged with other groups to form the multiracial Working People's Alliance (WPA). The WPA became a political party in 1979. ASCRIA filled a void in the society similar to how the National Joint Action Committee, NJAC, and Black Consciousness organizations also did throughout the world of that time.

3. *Caribbean Contact*, a weekly newspaper published in Barbados, was often the sole voice of unbiased news of the region.

5—ROBERT HILL / New York City, 2007

1. *Life and Debt* is a documentary film directed by Stephanie Black on the debt crisis in Jamaica during the 1980s.

2. Groundations is used synonymously with groundings, but is more often used to describe the expanded ritual described in paragraph one.

3. *Groundings with My Brothers,* Walter Rodney's first book, is a collection of his speeches published by Bogle L'Ouverture Press in London in 1968.

4. The protest became known as the "Rodney Riots." A march begun by students from the University of the West Indies, Mona, Kingston, on October 18, 1968, turned into a violent confrontation between police and youths, resulting in extensive property damage and three deaths.

5. Dr. Patricia Rodney, the wife of Dr. Walter Rodney.

6. A Guyanese-born writer of the Harlem Renaissance period, Eric Walrond is best known for his novel *Tropic Death* (New York: Boni & Liveright, 1926).

7. Dr. Lucille Mathurin Mair (née Walrond) later served as Jamaica's ambassador to Cuba and secretary general to the UN, Decade of Women. Dr. Mathurin-Mair is a historian with a focus on Caribbean women. She wrote *The Rebel Woman in the British West Indies during Slavery* (Kingston: Institute of Jamaica Publications, 1975).

8. The Institute of the Black World (IBW) in Atlanta once held the papers of Dr. Martin Luther King Jr. and served as a think tank on Pan-African issues.

9. William Strickland, professor of political science at the University of Massachusetts, Amherst, is a founding member of the IBW.

6—AMIRI BARAKA / Newark, New Jersey, 2009

1. Abdulrahman Mohamed Babu formed part of the unification team that brought Zanzibar and Tanganyika together as Tanzania. He served as Foreign Minister in the Julius Nyerere government of Tanzania.

2. The Sixth Pan-African Congress was held in Dar es Salaam in June 1974.

3. Amilcar Cabral was leader of the nationalist movement of Guinea-Bissau and Cape Verde Islands through the war of independence. He was assassinated by a rival on January 20, 1973, just eight months before Guinea-Bissau's declaration of independence. He is widely regarded as a strategist and revolutionary thinker. His ideas on the relationship between revolution and culture remain timely.

4. UNITA, National Union for the Total Independence of Angola, fought for independence against Portugal and later fought a bloody civil war against the MPLA. UNITA was supported by the United States and South Africa and came to represent the evil afflicting Africa. UNITA has since renounced violence and participates in electoral politics with limited success.

5. MPLA, People's Movement for the Liberation of Angola, led Angola's struggle for independence from Portugal and has ruled the country ever since.

6. TANU, Tanganyika African National Union, headed by Julius Nyerere, led the country to independence from Britain. In 1964, Tanganyika merged with Zanzibar and formed Tanzania.

7. FRELIMO, Liberation Front of Mozambique, led its country's war of liberation against Portugal and succeeded in 1975.

8. ANC, African National Congress, led the fight against apartheid in South Africa.

9. The National Black Political Convention was held in Gary, Indiana, March 10–12, 1972. It brought together a varied group of African American leaders that included elected officials and activists, integrationists and black nationalists, Baptists and Muslims. Coretta Scott-King and Betty Shabazz attended. The purpose was to plot an agenda for a way forward for African Americans.

10. The Congress of African People was intended to internationalize the African American struggle in the United States. Amiri Baraka sent an invitation to Walter to come from Tanzania to the conference.

11. Owusu Sadaukai led the movement to stage African Liberation Day, which morphed into the African Liberation Support Committee, where he served as national chairman.

12. Stokely Carmichael, now known as Kwame Toure, is credited with coining the phrase "Black Power."

13. Early on Sunday, July 23, 1967, the Detroit rebellion started after a confrontation with club patrons and the police. President Lyndon B.

Johnson called in the army, and Governor George Romney ordered the Michigan National Guard to intervene. It lasted for five days and resulted in 43 dead, 467 injured, over 7,200 arrests, and more than 2,000 buildings destroyed.

14. The Newark rebellion began on July 12, 1967. Again, the National Guard was called in and patrolled along with state and local police. The result: 23 dead, 700 injured, acres of property burned.

15. On August 11, 1965, a routine traffic stop in Watts, in south Los Angeles, escalated into a full-scale rebellion that lasted six days. More than thirty-four people died, with 1,000 wounded and an estimated $50 million to $100 million in property damage. The whole black world had been tense after Malcolm X's assassination in February 1965.

16. Rosa Parks is credited with igniting the bus boycott in Montgomery, Alabama, after refusing to give up her seat to a white man, as was the custom. She was arrested, and the boycott that followed resulted in the desegregation of the Montgomery bus service, but not before Dr. Martin Luther King Jr.'s home in Montgomery had been bombed.

17. The Black Power Conference of Newark, New Jersey, was held in July 1967 and is recorded as the first Black Power conference.

18. The Peoples' Revolutionary Constitutional Conference was held during the Labor Day weekend of 1970 at Temple University in Philadelphia. An estimated 8,000 radical civil rights activists and party supporters showed. The Black Panther Party hosted the convention.

19. J. Edgar Hoover served as head of the Federal Bureau of Investigation, which instituted COINTELPRO, a counterintelligence program designed to destroy progressive movements in the United States.

20. Condoleezza Rice served as secretary of state under President George W. Bush. She was the first African American female to serve in that position.

21. Colin Powell was the first African American in several high-profile U.S. government posts. He served as national security advisor, commander of the U.S. Army Forces Command, chairman of the Joint Chiefs of Staff, and secretary of state to President George W. Bush. When questioned about his record on civil rights, President Bush reportedly remarked, "What about Condi and Colin?" Quoted in Clarence Lusane, *Colin Powell and Condoleezza Rice: Foreign Policy, Race, and the New American Century* (Santa Barbara, CA: ABC-CLIO, 2006).

22. Richard Dean Parson served as CEO of Time Warner from 2003 to 2007 and is credited with turning the company around. He is currently chairman of the board at Citigroup.

23. Rev. Jesse Jackson electrified U.S. politics when he ran for the presidency in 1984 and 1988.

24. President Obama did not use public funds in his first bid for the White House.

7—LEITH MULLINGS / New York City, 2007

1. Dar es Salaam is the capital of Tanzania and home to the University of Dar es Salaam. Walter Rodney taught at the university, UDSM, from the beginning of the school year in 1967 to early 1968. He returned in 1970 and taught until 1974.
2. Mwalimu Julius Nyerere became premier of Tanganyika in 1961. When Tanganyika gained independence from the British in 1962, he became president. Tanganyika and Zanzibar united in 1964 to form Tanzania.
3. Yale University, New Haven, Connecticut.
4. Dr. C. Eric Lincoln served as professor emeritus of religion and culture at Duke University in Durham, North Carolina, where he taught from 1976 to 1993. He authored or coauthored over twenty books on the African American experience.
5. William Edward Burghardt Du Bois, born February 23, 1868, died August 27, 1963, is an intellectual giant known throughout the world and wrote several treatises on African American history and Pan-Africanism.
6. Immanuel Wallerstein, *The Modern World-System* (New York: Academic Press, 1974).

8—ISSA G. SHIVJI / At Home, Dar es Salaam, Tanzania, 2008

1. The Arusha Declaration is a manifesto that offers guidelines for the practice of a brand of ethics that promotes equality and mutual respect informed by African history and culture.
2. University of London, School of African and Oriental Studies.
3. Professor Issa G. Shivji currently serves in the Mwalimu Julius Nyerere Chair in Pan-African Studies, University of Dar es Salaam.
4. Frantz Fanon, a Martinique-born, French trained psychiatrist, described the psyche of oppression and the coming revolution in his books.
5. Osagyefo Kwame Nkrumah was Ghana's first president, founder of the Non-Aligned Movement, and a father in the Pan-African movement.
6. Samir Amin, noted Egyptian economist and head of CODESRIA, based in Dakar, Senegal.
7. Paul A. Baran, Stanford University professor of economics known for his Marxist views, wrote *The Political Economy of Growth* (New York: Monthly Review Press,1957).
8. Paul M. Sweezy, a Marxist economist, political activist, publisher, editor, and founder of the magazine *Monthly Review*.
9. Lancaster House, situated in West London and once part of St. James's Palace, is used by the foreign affairs department to host talks. It hosted the Zimbabwe independence talks as well as Guyana's.

10. *The Nationalist*, in its December 13, 1969, editorial quoting Rodney's paper said, "The Paper stated that 'armed struggle is the inescapable and logical means of obtaining freedom' and that independence which was achieved peacefully could not, by definition, be real independence for the masses." Reprinted in *Chemchemi: Fountain of Ideas* 3 (April 2010).

11. Born in Mozambique, Eduardo Mondlane attended college and graduate school in the United States. He returned to the region and was elected president of the Mozambique Liberation Front (FRELIMO), which was formed in Tanzania, and served until his assassination in 1969. After independence in 1975, the university in the Mozambique's capital, Maputo, was renamed Eduardo Mondlane University.

12. Ahmed Gora Ebrahim served as secretary of the PAC's department of foreign affairs. The Pan-African Congress was seen as a "black onsciousness" prong in the movement to end apartheid in South Africa.

13. Cheddi Jagan was the first premier of Guyana and led the movement for independence through the People's Progressive Party (PPP). The party split in 1955. Forbes Burnham led the exodus and formed the People's National Congress (PNC). With assistance from the United States and Britain, Burnham became premier in 1964 and led the negotiations for Guyana's independence, which came in 1966.

14. Kenyan freedom fighter Oginga Odinga served briefly as vice president under Jomo Kenyatta but resigned after differences with him. He continued in political life despite being jailed and often detained by Kenyatta and his successors.

15. The Narodniks represented a school of thought that originated in Russia sometime in the 1860s. They saw the peasantry as the revolutionary class that would overthrow the monarchy, and the village commune as the embryo of socialism, but believed the peasantry required a middle class or its equivalent to help engineer the revolution.

16. Ujamaa is the term for Mwalimu Julius Nyerere's view on socialism as applied to Africa.

17. Zimbabwe African National Union (ZANU).

18. Chris Hani, a lifelong member of the African National Congress in South Africa, was assassinated in 1993 by right-wing opponents of the ongoing negotiations to end apartheid. Hani once headed the ANC's military wing, Umkhonto we Sizwe.

19. Chitepo, a huge figure in the Zimbabwe liberation struggle and the Zimbabwe African National Union (ZANU) in particular, died on March 18, 1975, in Lusaka, Zambia; when a car bomb exploded. It killed him, his driver, and a neighbor. He was the first black African qualified as a barrister in (then-named) Rhodesia.

9—CLIVE YOLANDE THOMAS / Georgetown, Guyana, September 2007

1. Congress of Black Writers (1968), Montreal, Canada. Walter left Jamaica to attend the conference and was barred from returning to his job at the University of the West Indies..

2. Ralph Gonsalves was president of the Students' Guild at UWI, Mona, Jamaica, at the time of Walter Rodney's banning and is the current prime minister of Saint Vincent and the Grenadines.

3. Clive Y. Thomas, *Dependence and Transformation: The Economics of the Transition to Socialism* (New York: Monthly Review Press, 1974).

4. Dr. Joshua Ramsammy was an activist in groups like Movement Against Oppression (MAO) and Ratoon. These groups predated, then merged into, the Working People's Alliance (WPA). Ramsammy survived an assassination attempt that resulted in a bullet piercing his lung.

5. Prof. Clive Thomas wrote a series of articles for the *Sunday Edition, Stabroek News*.

6. In a statement released a few days after the assassination, the brother of Walter Rodney, Donald Rodney, said it was Gregory Smith who gave him the walkie-talkie that exploded, killing Walter.

7. Moses Bhagwan, WPA activist and attorney-at-law, founded the Ratoon group and published the WPA organ *Dayclean*.

8. The local telephone company, Guyana Telecommunications Corporation.

9. Gregory William Smith and Anne R. Wagner, *Assassination Cry of a Failed Revolution* (Bloomington, IN: Xlibris, 2007). Anne Wagner is Smith's sister.

10. Brickdam Cathedral, a centrally located landmark church operated by Jesuits.

11. To enter a country with inspection by immigration authorities.

12. In 1979, Maurice Bishop led a coup to overthrow the Grenada government of Eric Gairy.

13. A WPA activist and close confidant of Walter Rodney.

14. Michael Manley, former prime minister of Jamaica.

15. A Guyana Defense Force military plane.

10—RUPERT ROOPNARAINE / Georgetown, Guyana, 2007

1. In February 1980, Walter Rodney left Guyana for Zimbabwe. He also visited Tanzania and other countries in Africa and Europe. There is some dispute as to whether he was in Zimbabwe the same time as Forbes Burnham; that is, during the Zimbabwe independence celebrations. However, those who speak of his presence in Zimbabwe far outnumber any alternate views.

2. Patricia Rodney is Walter Rodney's wife
3. Eusi Kwayana a senior member of the WPA.
4. In February 1980, Dési Bouterse led a successful coup that overthrew the government of Johan Ferrier and declared Suriname a socialist republic.
5. "Leaderless" is a form of organization that allows cells consisting of as few as a single person to operate in the interest of the movement without a direct identifiable hierarchical structure.
6. William Gregory Smith and Anne R. Wagner, *Assassination Cry of a Failed Revolution* (Bloomington, IN: Xlibris, 2007). Here Smith writes that he gave the bomb to Walter Rodney's brother Donald, and that Walter Rodney knew the package contained a bomb. Donald Rodney gave a sworn statement in which he stated he believed the package contained a walkie-talkie.
7. CARICOM is a community of Caribbean nations bound by treaties to advance the region through cooperation. It was intended as a replacement for the failed West Indian Federation, but it too appears on its knees and headed for failure.
8. Ewart Thomas is currently a professor of psychology at Stanford University and from boyhood was a close friend of Walter Rodney.
9. University College of the West Indies later became University of the West Indies, Mona, Jamaica.
10. University of London, School of Oriental and African Studies.
11. Students in Cornell University's Afro-American Society occupied Willard Straight Hall in April 1969 and ended the occupation by streaming out with guns in hand. But they were mostly shotguns and hunting rifles, no AK47s.
12. A scholarship awarded to the best performing high school student in the country at the General Certificate of Education "A" (Advanced) level, prepared by the University of London.
13. The People's Progressive Party (PPP) often held meetings hosted by Rodney's father, Percival Rodney, and participants included both Cheddi Jagan and Forbes Burnham. This would have been before the split of 1955 that led to Burnham forming the People's National Congress (PNC).
14. General Vasco Gonçalves, an engineer by training, was decorated for service in Mozambique and Angola before returning home to become one of the leaders of the "Carnation Revolution" that overthrew dictator Marcello Caetano. Under this new government, Portugal ended its colonial wars and signed independence treaties with Angola, Mozambique, São Tomé and Principe, and Cape Verde. Portugal also withdrew from East Timor.
15. Otelo Saraiva de Carvalho, recognized as the chief strategist of the Carnation Revolution, was born in Mozambique of mixed Indian and

Portuguese heritage. His ancestry was reportedly from Goa, the South India resort town used as a trading port by the Portuguese since the sixteenth century. He was placed in charge of Command of the Continent (COPCON) and was instrumental in rebuffing the advances of the counterrevolutionary right wing of the armed forces.

16. *The Terror and the Time,* a film produced and directed by the Victor Jara Collective, of which Rupert Roopnaraine was a prominent member.

17. Deryck Murray, a cricketer from Trinidad and Tobago, represented the West Indies in sixty-two tests between 1963 and 1980. This period spanned the team's reign as the best in the world.

18. South Ruimveldt Gardens, known as "South," is a housing development in South Georgetown that was initially populated by a growing middle class, including many who had returned from study abroad. This is where Rodney lived on his return to Guyana in the 1970s.

19. Gregory Smith is alleged to have given Walter Rodney the package that contained the walkie-talkie that later exploded in the car, killed Walter, and wounded his brother Donald. A statement given by a frequent visitor to Smith's, Pamela Beharry, and published in the *Catholic Standard,* indicated that Smith was a member of the Guyana Defense Force, that he repaired radios and other electronic equipment, and that he had pulled a gun and threatened at least one neighbor. *Assassination Cry of a Failed Revolution,* by Smith and his sister Anne Wagner, recounts an incident where Smith shot and killed a man, as well as other attempts to kill him in French Guiana where he lived and died.

20. Executed not far from his home in "South" by police who alleged he was transporting weapons.

21. Edward Dublin sometimes served as bodyguard to Walter Rodney on trips to Linden. Dublin was executed by police in Linden, who alleged he had stolen building materials from a construction site.

22. Rickey Singh, a journalist for the *Guyana Chronicle* and *Caribbean Contact,* wrote often, and usually alone, in opposition to the dictatorial Burnham government.

23. Dr. Patricia Rodney (née Henry) is the widow of Walter Rodney and recently retired head of the Department of Public Health, Morehouse College.

24. A bowler in cricket is the equivalent to a pitcher in baseball except that the bowler runs to the pitching area and delivers the ball in one action.

25. The grammar school they attended divided the students into houses usually named after former teachers. Students would compete in all available competitions including cricket. But representing the school required that you excel beyond the houses.

26. Andaiye was a member of the inner circle of the WPA and confidante to Walter Rodney.

27. Karen DeSouza, active in the WPA, currently serves along with Andaiye in Red Thread, an organization dedicated to improving the lives of women and children in Guyana.

28. A village on the East Coast of Demerara. Though called the east coast because of the river, it faces north and runs along the Atlantic Coast of the country.

29. In 2007 Roopnaraine presented at the C. L. R James Lecture Series in Trinidad. In that lecture he responded to a lecture given in 1981 by C. L. R. James entitled, *Walter Rodney and the Question of Power* (London:Race and Class Publications, 1981). James's lecture was very critical of Walter's, and the WPA's, security arrangements and their understanding of revolution as the seizure of power.

30. Yuweri Museveni, current president of Uganda and former student of Rodney's while at the University of Dar es Salaam.

31. The New Jewel Movement (NJM), led by Maurice Bishop, formed in 1973 and overthrew Grenada dictator Eric Gairy in 1979. Bishop established close ties to Cuba, which helped Grenada build a new airport, among other infrastructure. Bishop was executed in 1983 by fellow party members. This incident triggered an all-too-ready U.S. invasion of Grenada, which many feel represented another turning point in Caribbean history, instigating the move toward neoliberalism.

32. The National Joint Action Committee (NJAC) formed in Trinidad and Tobago in 1969 for Black Power advocacy and was instrumental in the rising level of militancy and calls for racial unity in the fight against increased state repression. Led by Makandal Daaga, NJAC provided a background against which the 1970 mutiny almost led to the overthrow of the Eric Williams government. Today, Daaga is part of the People's Partnership coalition government.

33. Horace Campbell is currently professor of African-American studies, Syracuse University.

34. Winston James is associate professor of history, Columbia University.

INDEX